# CITIZENSHIP VALUES under the CONSTUTITION

# CITIZENSHIP VALUES under the CONSTUTITION

## Operationalisation and Teaching

*Editor*

**Subhash C. Kashyap**

**Citizenship Development Society**

*Co-Publisher*

GYAN

Citizenship Values under the Constutition



ISBN : 978-81-212-1177-2



Published in 2013 in India by
Gyan Publishing House
23, Main Ansari Road, Daryaganj,
New Delhi - 110002
Phones : 23282060, 23261060
Fax : (011) 23285914
E-mail: books@gyanbooks.com
website: gyanbooks.com

*Laser Type Setting :* Rajender Vashist, Delhi
*Printed at :* Chawla Offset Printers, Delhi

# Contents

# Preface

IN our polity, the role and responsibilities of citizens are enormous. We have not only rights but also obligations flowing from citizenship. Democracy ordains citizens active participation in the process of governance. For, in India's representative parliamentary democracy, the citizens are presumed to be ruling over themselves through their elected representatives.

The Constitution of India which we, the people, gave to ourselves, is not merely a political or legal document, it is above all a charter of citizenship values. Citizenship values under the Constitution imply all the rights, responsibilities and duties of citizens embodied in the Preamble, Fundamental Rights, Directive Principles and Fundamental Duties.

Justice Ranganath Mishra, former Chief Justice of India and then Chairman of the Citizenship Development Society (CDS) wrote a letter to the Chief Justice of India on 18th March, 1998, expressing serious concern at the Fundamental Duties of Citizens having remained only in the book; the Constitution having in fact "brought about a rights oriented society" with "the Indian approach of ensuring rights through performance of one's duties" having been totally abandoned.

Justice Mishra pointed out that "as a nation-building measure, teaching Fundamental Duties in every educational institution and as a measure of in-service training everywhere" was necessary as these "cannot be inculcated in our citizens unless these are brought into their minds and living process through teaching and education." Also, "it is the obligation of the State to educate the citizens in the matter of Fundamental Duties so that a right balance between rights and duties may emerge."

Contesting the petition, the Government of India in its affidavit happily supported the prayer made in the petition. A committee was set up by the Government of India (Ministry of Human Resource Development) to operationalise the suggestions to teach fundamental duties to the citizens of the country. Significantly enough, the Committee was headed by the then Chairman of CDS, Justice J.S. Verma, Former Chief Justice of India and two of its other four members (Dr. L.M. Singhvi and Dr. Subhash C. Kashyap) were from among members of the Governing Council of CDS.

The Verma Committee took note of the "work done by the Citizenship Development Society in the area of citizenship values" and decided to entrust to the Society the preparation of a Handbook on operationalisation of citizenship values under the Constitution.

The handbook with contributions from distinguished educationists, administrators, jurists and political scientists prepared by CDS was included in the report of Justice Verma Committee. Later, with the consent of Government of India, Ministry of HRD, the handbook was published as an independent CDS publication.

Dr K.B. Lall the then, President of the CDS in his preface to the handbook said that it was "a first step to provide a launching pad for a wide movement to comprehend the full import of Fundamental Rights and duties, to initiate action programmes, to transform mindsets prevailing in different walks of life and to enable all our citizens to realize their full potential".

In the context of the pressing demands for its copies, it is now being published in a book format, with a view to ensuring wider circulation and lasting impact. The text has been suitably revised and edited without changing the narration or the contemporaneous character of facts or views. A new introductory general chapter on Citizenship Values under the Constitution has been added.

It is hoped the book would be well received and found useful by educationists, educational institutions, planners, policy makers, teachers, teacher training institutes, students, NGOs and all concerned citizens.

The publishers, Gyan Publishing House, deserves all appreciation and gratitude from the Citizenship Development Society and from the wide citizenry for promptly and tastefully bringing out this book.

New Delhi
26 January, 2012

**Subhash C. Kashyap**
*Editor*

# Fundamental Duties

[Part IVA
FUNDAMENTAL DUTIES]

**51A. Fundamental Duties**— It shall be the duty of every citizen of India-

(a) to abide by the Constitution and respect its ideals and institutions, the National Flag and the National Anthem;

(b) to cherish and follow the noble ideals which inspired our national struggle for freedom;

(c) to uphold and protect the sovereignty, unity and integrity of India;

(d) to defend the country and render national service when called upon to do so;

(e) to promote harmony and the spirit of common brotherhood amongst all the people of India transcending religious, linguistic and regional or sectional diversities; to renounce practices derogatory to the dignity of women;

(f) to value and preserve the rich heritage of our composite culture;

(g) to protect and improve the natural environment including forests; lakes, rivers, wild life and to have compassion for living creatures;

(h) to develop the scientific temper, humanism and the spirit of inquiry and reform;

(i) to safeguard public property and to abjure violence;

(j) to strive towards excellence in all spheres of individual and collective activity so that the nation constantly rises to higher levels of endeavour and achievement.

[(k) who is a parent or guardian to provide opportunities for education to his child or, as the case may be, ward between the age of six and fourteen years.][1]

1. Added by the Constitution (Eighty-sixth Amendment) Act, 2002, sec. 4 (w.e.f. 1.4.2010).

# PART I

# Introduction

### *K.B. Lall*

The Citizenship Development Society was founded in 1979. Over the years, the Society has endeavoured to arouse awareness of the importance of building up good citizens and organize programmes and activities to promote and foster citizenship values.

In a message of encouragement the President, he observed: "Citizenship is a solemn duty which every individual must discharge with due diligence and dedication. A responsible and vigilant citizenry plays a vital role in strengthening our democracy and I am glad to learn that Citizenship Development Society, through its various activities, is inculcating citizenship values among our people".

The main thrust of our programmes has been on Value Education to train school teachers and teacher educators in the techniques and processes of identifying and inculcating values in their students. We have also convened Seminars and Workshops to spread the message to Civil Servants and Bank employees and Sarpanches and Panchayat officials. Efforts have also been made to persuade citizens to protect environment and to inform consumers of the ways in which they can protect their legitimate interest. The Society has established a Centre on Research and Training in Citizenship Development (CRTC) for designing educational programmes and developing course materials.

While the Society has gained valuable experience in generating awareness of citizenship values and facilitating their application at various work places, the range and reach of the Society's activity have been very limited. The current conjuncture of social, economic and political forces calls for a movement which captures the imagination of masses and motivates all categories of citizens to abide by the provisions of the Constitution in performing their duties and exercising their rights.

We are grateful to Justice Verma Committee for giving us the task of preparing a Hand-Book to facilitate the Operationalisation and Teaching of Fundamental Duties to our Citizens. We have sought the help of eminent persons with practical experience to reflect on the problems and interact with one another in elaborating feasible solutions. We found the subject to be vast, complex and challenging. There was wide variation in the conditions and characteristics of different segments of citizens. Accordingly it was decided to divide the citizens into eight categories or target groups. Each category was taken up for detailed work by one or two eminent persons. They looked at the group profile, considered the importance for its members of practising specific citizenship values, and evolved some suggestions for training in the application of Fundamental Duties to their work. Their first drafts were considered in joint meetings. The final result of their painstaking effort is presented in the following chapters. It will hopefully provide adequate inputs for commencement of field work.

In the First Chapter Mr. J.N. Sharma and Dr. K.M. Gupta have addressed the goal of laying foundation of citizenship values at the primary stage of the educational ladder. The pedagogues don't agree about inclusion of citizenship concept in Elementary Education. Now that Elementary Education will be made compulsory throughout the country it is essential to consider how best the children at that level can be helped to imbibe the essence of the values and duties prescribed in the Constitution.

The NCERT has already brought out instructional modules on national symbols and value education. It should not be difficult to give students at primary level clear understanding of such basic values as cleanliness, punctuality, truthfulness. They can also be acquainted with the life and work of great leaders who inspired our freedom struggle, Advantage can be taken of their natural curiosity to develop their interest in understanding, preserving and protecting the surrounding environment.

A few governmental and non-governmental organisations are researching and developing techniques and methodologies for inculcating values in growing children. The Research and Development Wing of CDS has made significant contributions in this regard. A number of practical suggestions for promoting values through direct and indirect methods have been made by the authors. Through imaginative activities inside and outside the class room, children's responses and reflexes can be influenced to be in spontaneous readiness to conform to the requirements of several provisions of Article 51A.

A great deal depends on the ingenuity and dedication of teachers. A nation wide movement to train and honour primary school teachers as builders of future citizens, if launched with sincerity and purpose, can bring about impressive transformation in the opening decades of the new millennium.

In chapter Two, Dr. N.K. Ambasht and Mrs. Supta Das have examined the situation at the Secondary Level of Education. The National Policy of Education (NPE) 1986 identified the components of the "common core", and provided the basic framework and orientation of school curricula in the country. All educable duties have been incorporated in shcoool curriculum and explained in the Text-books. But curricular instructions and process have achieved only "limited success" in inculcating these duties in the personal behaviour of the pupils.

In the view of the authors, our educational system should provide for such programmes/activities as ensure that the pattern of behaviour expected of a good citizen gets ingrained into an individual pupil and becomes a natural part of his/her personality. Deliberate behaviour modification should be an essential ingredient of the educational process at the Secondary Level.

It is imperative that the pupil becomes conscious of both rights and duties and grows with the understanding that rights without obligations encourage arrogance and duties without rights give rise to a form of slavery.

To achieve these goals, a continuous dialogue between policy framers and educationists has been suggested. The dialogue is expected to consider and recommend: (a) curricular modifications; (b) changes in assessment procedures and certification processes and (c) substantive improvements in teacher preparation programmes.

In order to increase the effectiveness of the class room instructional process, a series of very valuable suggestions has been made to expose the students to stimulus response situations, to note their behaviour and to formulate remedial actions programmes. Different agencies in the educational process are exhorted to join hands in this creative task.

In Chapter Three, Prof. R.B. Jain paints a disturbing and disappointing picture of the environment in Higher Educational Institutions. He describes the youth in universities to be biologically adult but socially irresponsible, to be free from familial control and at the same time united to domestic responsibilities, idealistic in their approach and yet willing victims of exploitation by vested political interests. He draws attention to heterogeneity in the student body, comprising consequent indiscipline and unrest. The situation requires urgent steps to provide at the campuses systematic education in democratic citizenship.

Prof. Jain has traced the origin of the concept of citizenship, enumerated the citizenship values enshrined in the Constitution, analysed the osmotic relationship between rights and duties. He has suggested that both compulsory and optional orientation programmes be organised to spread knowledge about citizenship values and to foster their application to cultural, sports and trade union activities on the campus.

For the purpose of taking practical steps, three target groups need to be addressed. These are students, teachers and administrators. Urgent need to improve communication between them has been emphasised. It will be useful to identify in all organised activities, focal points for application of specific Fundamental Duties and for overseeing and monitoring their implementation. Several interesting suggestions have been made for organising extra-curricular activities to provide opportunities to student participants to learn to discharge their obligations towards the institutions to which they belong and towards the community of citizens in general.

Since University students constitute the most dynamic and progressive component of citizenry, a series of initiatives must be urgently undertaken to move their minds in the direction of compliance with Fundamental Duties.

In the Fourth Chapter, Shri J. Veera Raghvan focuses his attention on democratic governance by People's Representatives from Panchayats to Parliament. They have the same rights and duties as other fellow citizens. However, as leaders and exemples, their responsibility is much greater. Those who take a specific oath are bound by its terms to practice and propagate the culture of the Constitution. The elected representatives have a major role in ensuring that Fundamental Duties become a living reality for the elite as also for our masses.

In particular, the candidates seeking the mandate of the people must eschew arousing sectarian passions and take all practical steps to promote national unity and integrity. It is their duty to propagate the noble ideals which inspired the struggle for freedom, to sustain self-reliance, foster scientific temper, recognize merit and stimulate the urge towards excellence. Their success depends on productive service to their constituency and not on distributing public revenues in an unproductive fashion.

While taking proper action to secure redressal of grievances, elected representatives should refrain from interfering in the functioning of governmental and non-governmental institutions. They should observe the laws themselves and help law enforcing agencies in dealing with law breakers; they should adhere to their DHARMA which is a compound of selflessness, integrity, objectivity, accountability, openness, honesty and leadership.

It should be the endeavour of elected representatives to organize/strengthen a network of activities to gather support for small families, to protect and improve natural environment, to safeguard public property and abjure violence.

The environment in which elected representatives function is full of contradictions and complexities. They can lead the country to genuine progress through balance and moderation. They must always strive to act in the larger interest of the country and in accordance with their conscience.

Orientation Programmes are being organised for new Members of Parliament. Similar programmes have been instituted at the level of State Legislatures. Training Courses have also been devised for the benefit of the Elected Representatives serving Municipal and Panchayati Raj Institutions. These programmes need to be strengthened to provide an adequate measure of understanding of Fundamental Duties and their application to the work of elected representatives.

In Chapter Five, Mr. S.B. Lal directs his attention to Public Servants. He puts their strength at two crores. They play a crucial role in national life. They undertake a wide range of tasks including maintenance of law and order, enforcement of socially beneficial regulations, implementation of development programmes and ensuring a level playing field. They are catalytic agents of change and their activities affect the lives of citizens in a variety of ways. If they sincerely apply the quintessence of fundamental Duties to the performance of their appointed tasks, they would not only serve as worthy examples for fellow citizens but also succeed in bringing about immense improvement in the quality of their lives.

Fortunately, adequate arrangements exist for the training of different categories of Civil Servants. Mr. Lal has drawn up broad outlines of a MODEL MODULE to be adopted for inclusion in the Courses of different training institutions for teaching the trainees Fundamental Duties and Values as enshrined in the Constitution and for helping them to mould their behaviour accordingly. The duty cast on Civil Servants to strive towards excellence will enable them to attain higher ethical standards and make up the deficits in several areas of democratic governance.

Every Public Servant should be administered a pledge to abide by the provisions of the Constitution and carry out fully the Fundamental Duties prescribed therein. It is suggested that suitable systems and procedures be instituted in all Departments to ensure that the pledge is implemented, all administrative activity is transparent and accountable, and corrupt practices are effectively eliminated.

In Chapter Six, Shri K.V. Viswanathan looks closely and critically at the Administration of Justice. Although he finds the prevailing system to be sound and time tested, he fears it is deteriorating fast. It has been, he feels, corrupted and abused, even by those who are primarily responsible for its efficacy and probity. Inadequate commitment on the part of the citizenry to perform Fundamental Duties is largely to be blamed for this sorry state of affairs. In his view, the process of its degeneration can be reversed if

CITIZENS become aware of the importance of complying with the "Ten Commandments" in Article 51A of the Constitution. The Supreme Court has set the trend in adopting the Fundamental Duties as yardsticks for testing the correctness of laws and actions by those who administer them.

Target Groups for spreading the above message have been identified. Detailed steps which may be advantageously taken by teachers and students in Law Colleges have been spelt out. Bar Councils and their affiliated Bar Associations must share the responsibility for ensuring that their members not only appreciate the value of complying with Fundamental Duties but also strive to implement them while pursuing their professional work.

It has been suggested that Judicial Academy should be set up to provide facilities for continuing education of Judges, to focus their attention on constitutional values and Fundamental Duties, to foster constructive interaction between the Bar and the Bench and to facilitate application of modern techniques of management to the transaction of judicial business in the Courts.

In Chapter Seven, Prof. Brij Mohan and Dr. D.N. Saxena bring into focus the role of business and industry sector in operationalising Fundamental Duties. This Sector accounts for more than fifty percent of the Net Domestic Product. While it is a part of the social system, it contributes to the value base of the social order. When it has a long term perspective, it adopts upright practices. When it concentrates on maximising short term gains, it cuts corners and gets entrapped in unethical conduct.

Business carries out its gainful operations under the umbrella of Fundamental Rights guaranteed in the Constitution. It has the corresponding obligation to perform the duties, both implicit and explicit, enjoined by the Constitution. However, in discharging social responsibilities only, a small percentage of the business community has undertaken social welfare and development programmes. Important Chambers of Commerce and Industry Associations have taken initiative for formulating norms of ethical conduct for business dealings. But the action taken to secure compliance with the codes leaves much to be desired.

This sad state of affairs is due to the low level of public awareness of the duties the citizens owe to the State, the society and the fellow citizens. As far back as 1987, the Citizenship Development Society drew attention to this aspect in the Bangalore Declaration adopted by the National Seminar held in collaboration with the Gokhale Institute of Public Affairs. In his book "Citizens and the Constitution" Dr. Kashyap has discussed in depth the basic values embedded in the Preamble and parts III and IV of the Constitution, as also the Fundamental Duties prescribed in its Article 51A. These together with other publications by CDS provide inputs for a systematic campaign to spread knowledge and understanding by businessman and business entities of their constitutional obligations.

Business leaders, business organisations and Management Schools have vital roles to play in internalising basic values, in widening financial and technical support for community development programmes, and in ensuring that ethical codes become indispensable ingredients of business ethos. If in the strategy of operationalising Fundamental Duties, a priority is accorded to achieving excellence in all individual and collective activity to nurturing the scientific temper and imbibing the spirit of enquiry and reform the national economy, itwill soon scale new heights.

In Chapter Eight, Mr. Prem Kumar makes out a strong case for Value Based Media. The traditional role ascribed to media which includes television and radio is to inform, educate and entertain the people. It wields immense power to influence public opinion and rouse individual consciousness. Lime all forces this power can be used for both constructive and destructive purposes.

Media derives its prowess from Article 19(1) of the Constitution which guarantees to all citizens the right to freedom of speech and expression. Although most of the media is in private hands, whileperforming vital public functions.

Media's right to freedom is subject to reasonable restrictions on the grounds set out in Articles19 (2) and (6) of the Constitution. It has also the corresponding duty to refrain from trenching on the rights of other citizens or jeopardising public interest. A statutory Press Council of India has been established with the object of preserving freedom of the press and overseeing proper professional conduct by those engaged in the profession of journalism. There are guidelines and codes of conduct for those engaged in other media functions. These codes serve to curb negative tendencies in the Media.

However, the media seems to be unaware of the Fundamental Duties laid down in Article 51A or the VALUES enshrined in the Preamble and Articles 36 to 51 of the Constitution. It is the duty of those engaged in Media to repair this omission urgently. These Duties and Values are as binding on Media as on all other citizens, Media's constituent bodies should consider and adopt ways to implement Fundamental Duties in the course of their operations.

Media also has broader social obligations. It can use its facilities to pursue the positive purpose of explaining to fellow citizens the true intent of each of the Fundamental Duties and assisting them in mobilising and monitoring their endeavours to give practical effect to the values enshrined in the Constitution.

There is no provision in the Constitution for the enforcement of Fundamental Duties. And yet without compliance with Duties, Fundamental Rights cannot be enjoyed. Duties are inseparable from Rights. Neither can be taught in isolation. The two together constitute

Citizenship Values on which rests the well-being of our democratic polity.

These values have a moral quality and an ethical dimension. It is imperative to make them a part of our being, individual and collective, to ensure that they regulate our behaviour and govern our conduct. In obedience to the mandate from the Justice Verma Committee, earnest efforts have been made to identify the values relative to each area of study, to propose ways for disseminating their knowledge, to discuss their application to live situations and to put forward suggestions for overseeing their operationalisation. The outcome of these efforts is submitted as a first step to provide a launching pad for a nation wide MOVEMENT to comprehend the full import of Fundamental Rights and Duties, to initiate action programmes to transform mind sets prevailing in different walks of life and enable all our CITIZENS to realize their full potential.

The Citizenship Development Society will feel privileged if it is given an opportunity to play an appropriate role in this Movement.

# List of Contributors

**Subhash C. Kashyap**, Former Secretary General, Lok Sabha.

**J.N. Sharma**, Former Deputy Commissioner, Kendriya Vidyalaya Sangathan.

**K.K. Gupta**, Former Reader, Department of Education, NCERT.

**N.K. Ambasht**, Former Chairman, National Institute of Open Schooling.

**Supta Das**, Lecturer, Department of Social Sciences and Humanities, NCERT.

**R.B. Jain**, Prof., Department of Public Administration, University of Delhi.

**J. Veeraraghavan**, Chairman, K.M. Munshi Institute, Bhartiya Vidya Bhavan.

**S.B. Lal**, Retired Secretary, Government of India.

**K.V. Vishwanathan**, Senior Advocate, Supreme Court of India.

**Brij Mohan**, Dean, Indian Institute of Foreign Trade.

**D.N. Saxena**, Former, Jt. Secretary, Ministry of Finance and Director General, Indian Institute of Foreign Trade.

**Prem Kumar**, Senior journalist.

# Citizenship Values Under the Constitution

*Subhash C. Kashyap*

Citizenship Values Under Our Constitution are basically democratic values. Adult citizens elect their representatives to make laws and to form government. The ultimate responsibility, however, remains that of the citizens themselves. For, the rulers and the ruled are both primarily citizens.

The vibrancy of democratic politics is contingent upon the spread of education. The relationship between democracy and education is a reciprocal one. The importance of education acquiring and developing democratic citizenship values is unique. For, it is only an educated society that can be aware of its rights and duties, of citizenship values, of constitutional obligations, of national policies and the like.

Success of democratic polity depends only upon the kind and quality of citizenship it has. All the citizens of India are expected to be committed to the basic constitutional values and to make the Indian experiment with democracy successful. This is a stupendous responsibility and calls, first of all, for education in democracy and citizenship values and in the privileges and responsibilities of democratic citizenship.

An appropriate machinery ought to be created for teaching the ordinary voters their duties and responsibilities as citizens of India under democratic polity, Gandhi had said, "True swaraj is to be attained only by educating the masses to a sense of their capacity to regulate and control authority."

According to the Verma Committee, "creation of a citizenry conscious of citizenship values including their rights and duties and committed to the principles embodied in our Constitution is a prerequisite to social advancement, economic development and political progress of our country." Therefore, there is need to make conscious efforts to promote an awareness of the constitutional obligations among citizens. The committee further observed:

> "Article 51A comprises such aspects as cannot be ignored any more. These have to be paid immediate and urgent attention by the systems in existence as well as by the individuals in the society. Essentially all that is contained in the Fundamental Duties is just a codification of tasks integral to the Indian way of life. A close scrutiny of the clauses of Article 51A would indicate that number of these clauses basically refer to such values as have been a part of the Indian tradition, mythology, religions and practices. At this juncture of history, the nation realizes an urgent need to re-emphasize these in a manner that would be acceptable to and be imbibed by all generations. To achieve these objectives, it would be essential to create public awareness of the need to appreciate and internalize the concept and practice of Fundamental Duties with particular emphasis on the necessity of creating a harmonious society with a scientific outlook, free from tensions and turmoils".

Fundamental Duties of citizens seek to emphasize such fine moral qualities and values as virtue, culture, a sense of discipline, a strong sense of social responsibility, a historical mission, a spirit of self-sacrifice, a creative and pioneering spirit, being capable of working for the interests of the vast majority of society and understanding, showing concern for and helping others. Fundamental Duties help the citizens in forming ideals, studying assiduously, seeking truth and striving to make progress, treasuring nationalism, rising gallantly for righteousness, being courteous, magnanimous, faithful, and harmonising one's action to one's words.

Citizenship duties are not the duties of the people as against those of the Government. These are visualized as fundamental duties of citizens in Government as also of citizens at large. Those in Government lecturing others on citizenship duties are bound to be looked at with suspicion. Similarly, citizens always demanding their rights would appear to lack social consciousness.

## Enforceability of Duties

There is no provision in the Constitution for direct enforcement of the Fundamental Duties enshrined in Article 51A nor is there any provision to prevent their violation. But, as Justice Venkataramiah pointed out, there is no provision declaring them non-justiciable either and in the context of the use of the terms 'fundamental' and 'duties', these should *prima facie* be enforceable. To ensure their effectuation, it is the obligation of legislatures to enact suitable laws. It may be expected that in determining the constitutionality of any law, if Supreme Court finds that it seeks to give effect to any of these Duties, it may consider such law to be "reasonable" in relation to article 14 or 19 and thus save such law from unconstitutionality.

## The Purpose of incorporating the Fundamental Duties

The purpose of incorporating the Fundamental Duties in the Constitution is to make the citizens aware of their obligations and to warn them to do and not to do certain things in the interests of their country, their fellow citizens and themselves.

As the Verma Committee said:

> "The Supreme Court of India has in several cases relied on Fundamental Duties contained in Article 51A to determine the duty of the State, and when necessary, give directions or frame guidelines to achieve the purpose. This has been done in several cases relating to preservation and conservation of environment, ecology and prevention of degeneration of forests, wild life, flora and fauna, etc. The court has observed that preservation of environment and maintenance of the ecological balance are the responsibility not only of the Government but also the Fundamental Duty of every citizen."

**The Eleven Duties**

Part IV A (Article 51A) lists eleven duties of citizenship:

**(i) Respect the Constitution, the Flag and the Anthem:** The first and the foremost duty assigned to every citizen of India is to abide by the Constitution and respect its ideals and institutions, the National flag and National Anthem. These are the very physical foundations of our citizenship. All of us are supposed to maintain the dignity of the Constitution by not indulging in any activities in violation of the letter or spirit of the Constitution. Ours is a vast country with many languages, sub-cultures and religious and ethnic diversities, but essential unity of the country is epitomized in one Constitution, one flag, one people and one citizenship. We are all governed and guided by this Constitution irrespective of caste, religion, race, sex, etc. The Constitution was the result of the many commitments, promises and pledges made by nationalist leaders to the people of India. Also, it embodied efforts at reconciliation, accommodation, and compromise. All of us and the Fundamental Rights of each of us are protected by it. Similarly, the National Flag and the National Anthem are symbols of our history, sovereignty, unity and pride. If a citizen of India by any overt or covert act shows disrespect to the Constitution, the National Anthem or National Flag, it would be not only an anti-social and anti-national activity but it would also spell doom to all our rights and our very existence as citizens of a sovereign nation. Each citizen must therefore not only refrain from any such activity but also do his best to prevent any miscreant trying to show disrespect to our national symbols. Every nation is proud of its citizens because of their dedication, sincerity and patriotism. We, the citizens of India, have to be equally proud of our nation, our Constitution, our Flag and our Anthem. We must put the nation above our narrow personal interests and then only we will be able to protect our hard-earned freedom and sovereignty.

**(ii) Cherish the ideals of the Freedom Struggle:** The citizens of India must cherish and follow the noble ideals which inspired the national struggle for freedom. The battle of freedom was a long one where thousands sacrificed their lives for our freedom. It becomes our duty to remember the sacrifices made by our forefathers for the cause of the country. But, what is much more important is to remember, imbibe and follow the ideals which pervaded our unique struggle. It was not a struggle merely for political freedom of India. It was for the social and economic emancipation of the people all over the world. Its ideals were those of building a just society and a united nation, of freedom, equality, non-violence, brotherhood and world peace. If we, the citizens of India, remain conscious of and committed to these ideals, we will be able to rise above the various fissiparous tendencies raising their ugly heads now and then, here and there. Parties and politicians who use religion, casteism, separatism, etc. for political ends and for capturing power are clearly violating their Fundamental Duties under the Constitution.

**(iii) Uphold sovereignty, unity and integrity of India:** To protect the sovereignty, unity and integrity of

India is a pre-eminent national obligation of all the citizens of India in a democratic system of governance. Sovereignty lies with the people. To defend our sovereignty is our own responsibility. If the freedom and unity of the country are jeopardized, the nation ceases to exist and if there is no nation, who lives?

It may be recalled that the values of sovereignty, unity and integrity of the nation are first mentioned in the Preamble to the constitution. Under Article 19(2) of the Fundamental Rights, reasonable restrictions are permitted on freedom of speech and expression in the interests of the "sovereignty and integrity of India".

**(iv) Defend the country and render National Service:** The primordial origins of the State are said to be in the need to defend ourselves against external enemies. In modern nation States, it is considered axiomatic that every citizen is bound to be ready to defend the country against war or external aggression. Present-day wars are not fought on the battlefield only nor are they won only by the armed forces; the citizens at large play a most vital role in a variety of ways. Sometimes civilians may be required also to take up arms in defense of the country, if the situation warrants it. By fighting to defend the country, the citizens are fighting only to defend their own liberty and that of their posterity.

Here, mention may be made of article 23(2) whereunder the State is allowed to impose "compulsory service for public purposes" subject to the condition that no discrimination is made on grounds of religion, race, caste or class or any of them.

**(v) Promote Harmony and Brotherhood**: To promote harmony and the spirit of common brotherhood amongst all the people of India essentially flows from the basic values of fraternity enshrined in the Preamble the Constitution. India is a country of different castes, languages, religions and many cultural streams, but we are one people with one

Constitution, one flag and one citizenship. The spirit of brotherhood should come very normally among the citizens of a country like India where the norm has been to consider the entire world as one family. The Constitution also casts upon us the Fundamental Duty of ensuring that all practices derogatory to the dignity of women are renounced. This again should come normally to a country where the ideals said that gods reside where women are worshipped (*yatra naryastu pujyante ramante tatra devata)*. It is for us to rise above the later day degenerations and aberrations which tarnished the image of our society. Incidentally, it may be noted that under article 23 (1) of the Fundamental Rights, traffic in human beings is prohibited.

**(vi) Preserve Rich Heritage of Composite Culture:** To preserve the rich heritage of our composite culture is another Fundamental Duty of every Indian citizen. Our cultural heritage is one of the noblest and the richest. Also, it is part of the heritage of the earth. What we have inherited from the past we must preserve and pass on to the future generations in tact. Each generation leaves its footprints on the sands of time. We must hold precious and dear what our forefathers created and their successive generations bequeathed to us as symbols of their artistic excellence and achievement. Generations to come always draw inspiration from past history which stimulates them to aim at ever greater heights or achievement and excellence. It becomes the ardent duty of every citizen to ensure that these monuments and pieces of art are not in any way damaged, disfigured, scratched or subjected to vandalism or greed of unscrupulous traders and smugglers.

One of the most ancient civilisations of the world, India can take legitimate pride in having been a civilisational unity without a break for more than five thousand years. We all are part of this great civilisation and culture. Our contributions in the field of art, sculpture, mathematics, science, medicine, etc., are well-known. Some of the oldest, deepest and most sublime philosophical thought and literature was born in India. We have several historical monuments of great archaeological value spread over the entire country. These include forts, palaces, temples, cave paintings, mosques, churches, etc. Also, this territory has the honour of being the birth place of several great religions like Hinduism, Buddhism, Jainism and Sikhism.

Our past has shown us the path of peace, love, non-violence and truth. As citizens of this country, it is the responsibility of us all to work for the preservation of this rich heritage and its cultural values, and live in love and harmony.

The Directive Principle, under article 49 similarly enjoin the State to protect monuments and places and objects of national, artistic or historic importance.

**(vii) Improve Environment:** In the face of the menace of the increasing pollution and environmental degradation, it is the duty of every citizen to protect and improve natural environment including forests, lakes, rivers and wild life and to have compassion for living creatures. The rising air, water and noise pollution and large-scale denudation of forests is causing immense harm to all human life on earth. The mindless and wanton deforestation in the name of the needs of development is causing havoc in the form of natural calamities and imbalances. By protecting our forest cover, planting new trees, cleaning rivers, conserving water resources, reforesting waste lands, hills and mountains and controlling pollution in cities, villages and industrial units, we can help save the future of our fellow citizens and of planet earth itself. What is needed is a concerted effort at an awareness campaign and a planned strategy to move forward through voluntary citizen initiatives. Governmental steps alone cannot help bring about a pollution-free atmosphere.

The mention of protection of environment etc. as a duty of citizens is intended to reinforce the other constitutional provision of Article 48A under the Directive Principles which enjoins the State to protect and improve the environment and safeguard the forests and wild life. Earth is the common heritage of man and animals. We have no right to annihilate or drive away the wild denizens from their territory or natural habitat. Ancient Indian thought talks of *Sarvesham Shantir bhavatu* (peace unto all living beings and entire environment) or *Ahimsa Paramodharma, Ahimsa paramotapah* (non-violence is the greatest duty and the greatest penance).

(For the large number of court cases directed at securing protection of the environment and prevention of pollution, see Annexure E (pp. 237-339) *in Vol. II, Report of the Committee on Fundamental Duties of Citizens,* GOI, Min. HRD, New Delhi, 1999).

**(viii) Develop Scientific Temper, Humanism etc :** One of our great founding fathers, Jawaharlal Nehru always laid treat emphasis on the need for Indian citizens developing a scientific temper and a spirit of inquiry-inquisitiveness for learning from developments around the world. This was particularly necessary because of the most revolutionary scientific advances made during this century and in the context of our background of superstitions, obscurantism and backwardness. In keeping with his views and concerns, Nehru laid the foundations of the modem industrialized India by building the necessary scientific and technological infrastructures. Now, it is the bounden duty of every citizen to preserve and promote a scientific temper and spirit of inquiry to keep pace with the fast changing world. Also, the Constitution ordains that Science and Technology must be tempered with a sense of humanism because ultimately the end of all progress is the human being and the quality of life and relationships that are developed.

**(ix) Safeguard Public Property and Abjure Violence:** It was most unfortunate that in a country which preached non-violence to the rest of the world, we saw from time to time spectacles of senseless violence and destruction of public property indulged in by a few of its citizens. This is why it was considered necessary to prescribe the responsibility "to safeguard public property and abjure violence" as a fundamental citizenship duty.

**(x) Strive for Excellence:** The drive for excellence in all spheres of individual and collective activity is the demand of times and a basic requirement in a highly competitive world. Nothing but the best would have survival potential in tomorrow's world. This would include respect for professional obligations and excellence. Whatever work we take up either as individual citizens or as groups, our effort should be directed to achieving the goal of excellence. Also, special emphasis is called for in the area of collective activity. It is often said that the performance of individual Indians is excellent but we lack team spirit. If this drawback can be remedied we can put India on the map as a fast developing country.

**(xi) Duty to educate Children:** New article 21A inserted by the Constitution (86th Amendment) Act, 2002 lays down that the State shall provide free and compulsory education to all children of the age of six to fourteen years. Alongwith making it a fundamental right the amendment also inserted in article 51A a new fundamental duty requiring every parent or guardian to provide opportunities for education to his child or ward between the age of six and fourteen years.

It hardly needs any arguing that each of these duties devolves on every citizen of India and more particularly on those citizens who happen to occupy positions of authority as rulers, administrators, legislators, judges or other high functionaries of the State. The Supreme Court has upheld the principle that since the duties are obligatory for all citizens, authorities of the State have also to observe them.

For the implementation of at least some of the fundamental duties of citizens, as the Verma Committee (1999) has stated, legal provisions exist:

(A) The Emblems and Names (Prevention of Improper Use) Act, 1950 was enacted soon after independence, *inter alia,* to prevent improper use of the National Flag and the National Anthem.

(B) In order to ensure that no disrespect is shown to the National Flag, Constitution of India and the National Anthem, the Prevention of Insults to National Honour Act, 1971 was enacted.

(C) In order to ensure that correct usage regarding display of the National Flag is well understood, the instructions issued from time to time on the subject have been embodied in *Flag Code India* which has been made available to all the State Governments and Union Territory Administrations (UTs).

(D) There are a number of provisions in the existing criminal laws to ensure that the activities which encourage enmity between different groups of people on grounds of religion, race, place of birth, residence, language, etc. are adequately punished. Writings, speeches, gestures, activities, exercises, drills, etc. aimed at creating a feeling of insecurity or ill-will among the members of other communities, etc. have been prohibited under Section 153A of the Indian Penal Code (IPC).

(E) Imputations and assertions prejudicial to national integration constitute a punishable offence under Section 153B of the IPC.

(F) A communal organisation can be declared unlawful association under the provisions of Unlawful Activities (Prevention) Act, 1967. Offences related to religion and castes are covered in Sections 295-298 of IPC (Chapter XV) and provision of the Protection of Civil Rights Act, 1955 (earlier the Untouchability (Offences)

Act, 1955). Section 123(3) and (3A) of the Representation of People Act, 1951 declares that soliciting of votes on the ground of religion, and promotion or attempt to promote feelings of enmity or hatred between different classes or citizens of India on grounds of religion, race, caste, community or language are corrupt practise. A person indulging in a corrupt practice can be disqualified from being a Member of Parliament or a State Legislature under Section 8A of the Representation of People Act.

The courts can certainly take fundamental duties of citizens into consideration while construing a law amenable to more than one interpretation. Article 51A(g) regarding protection of environment has particularly come up before the courts. Oral orders were issued by the Supreme Court for stopping quarrying operation in some areas in the State of U.P. Also, orders were issued in respect of declaring certain disputed areas as reserved forests under the Indian Forests Act, 1927.

The legislators Ministers, lawmakers and the administrators- have to be conscious not only of the Fundamental Duties of citizens at large but also of their own Fundamental Duties as citizens. It is one of their most fundamental constitutional obligations to be all the time aware of the Fundamental Rights of the whole mass of citizens under the Constitution. For, wherever an obligation is cast on the 'State', cast it is, on the citizens in position of authority to implement it. Implicit in the mandatory obligations of the State are the optional but indispensably positive obligations also of the private citizens at large.

Inasmuch as we are dependent on the Constitution of India and on the unity and integrity of the Indian nation for our continued status as citizens of India, it is our bounden duty not only to observe each of the Duties enumerated in Part IVA of the Constitution but also to respect meticulously and try to implement through every means at our disposal, our conduct and actions all the citizenship values explicit or implied under the Constitution.

Further, attempt made to tabulate the basic values of democratic citizenship as they emerge from provisions of the Constitution. Their quintessence may be put in capsule form or in the form of *sutras*:

- Sovereignty vests in the collectivity of citizens.
- Citizenship is indivisible.
- Unity and integrity of the nation constitute a sacred trust.
- All citizens are equal.
- Citizenship identity overrides all other identities.
- Respect freedom of faith and religion, profession, thought and expression, assembly and association, and residence and movement for all citizens.
- Cultivate mutual regard for all the Indian languages, scripts and rich heritage of our composite culture.
- Citizens in positions of power must conform to citizenship values in the discharge of their responsibilities.
- Fraternity provides basis for a democratic way of life abjuring violence and ensuring mutual respect, accommodation and cooperation.
- Self-discipline and democratic ethos go hand in hand.
- Franchise is both a right and a duty, participation in democratic processes is an obligation to fellow citizens.
- Elimination of illiteracy and promotion of education is essential ingredient of citizenship duties.
- Respect the Constitution, National Flag, National Anthem and the ideals of the freedom struggle.
- Develop scientific temper and cultivate humanism.
- Respect environment.

# PART II
# OPERATIONALISATION AND TEACHING

# 1

# Elementary Education: Foundation of Citizenship Values

*J.N. Sharma* and *K.M. Gupta*

We are at present faced with the challenge of breakdown of human values that threaten the stability of our society. It is strange and even tragic that after so many years of the independence we are still discussing the place of values in our education system. The consolation is that we have at least begun giving attention to this important subject; the National Policy on Education (NPE), 1986 also laid great emphasis on this issue. The basic aim of education is to produce men of knowledge as well as culture. There is always the danger of conveying knowledge in vacuum. Divorced from life, education will only become the means of mechanically conveying inert ideas.

The nation has made tremendous progress in all walks of life. The country has strived to achieve the goal of universalisation of elementary education. In the Directive Principles of State Policy of the Constitution of India, a commitment is reflected under article 45. The number of primary schools increased from 2.10 lakhs in 1951 to 7.36 lakhs in 1986 to 8.22 lakhs in 1993. Similarly, the number of upper primary school increased from 13,600 in 1951 to 1.36 lakhs in 1986 to 1.62 lakhs in 1993. The facilities for primary education are available to a large extent to all children in the country. Out of the total inhabitated villages 5,86,365 in the country more that 93% of them have facilities for primary education. The number of teachers in primary schools increased from 14,92,721 in 1986 to 16,23,379 in 1993. But we were yet not able to achieve the goal of universalisation of elementary education as envisaged in the Indian Constitution in 1950. Similarly, we were yet not able to educate our children in the provisions related with the Fundamental Duties as given in article 51A. Though we may believe in equality but it is not reflected in our behaviour. The National Policy on Education, 1986 as modified in 1992 clearly accepted the phenomena. We are conscious that India's political and social life is passing through a phase of erosion of long accepted values. The goals of secularism, socialism, democracy and professional ethics are coming under increasing strain. The facility for teaching about the Constitution of India is almost non-existent at elementary level. The pedagogues do not agree about inclusion of citizenship concept at the primary school level. The child has not attained the operational stage when he is in primary school. But if we see the ground reality a child is a keen witness to the interaction between parents. The mass media is continuously influencing a child. He watches regular and irregular behaviour of politicians. During this process he develops an understanding of the concepts like citizenship, equality, etc. But what is missing in the whole process is an Indian citizen or *Bhartiya Nagrik.*

### What does our Constitution Say?

The Preamble of our Constitution is the source of values. It is being reproduced here to understand the fundamental principles embodied in it. It states:

"WE, THE PEOPLE OF INDIA, having solemnly resolved to constitute India into a [SOVEREIGN SOCIALIST SECULAR DEMOCRATIC REPUBLIC] and to secure to all its citizens:

JUSTICE, Social, Economic and Political;

LIBERTY of thought, expression, belief, faith and worship;

EQULITY of status and of opportunity;

and to promote among them all

FRATERNITY assuring the dignity of the individual and [unity and integrity of the Nation];

IN OUR CONSTITUENT ASSEMBLY this twenty-sixth day of November, 1949, do HEREBY ADOPT, ENACT AND GIVE TO OURSELVES THIS CONSTITUTION."

There is no provision for teaching of Constitution either at the teacher training institutions or in the school curriculum. Even specific provisions related to fundamental duties are not referred in our curriculum. A preliminary knowledge about our National Flag, National Anthem and State Emblem is given in the curriculum at primary school level. The NCERT in its Programme of Mass Orientation for School Teachers (PMOST) included self-instructional modules on our national symbols (NCERT 1998). Similarly a module of value education is included in self-instructional package for Special Orientation Programme for Primary Teachers (NCERT 1995). These efforts have generated awareness among the teaching community. The Fundamental Duties enshrined in our Constitution under Article 51A are being discussed from the point of view of its implication for the teachers.

As teachers of elementary level, it is our responsibility to practise the values enshrined in the Indian Constitution. In day-to-day functioning of school, we should promote various ideas contained under Article 51A of the Fundamental Duties. As citizens, we are expected to carry out the above Fundamental Duties prescribed in the Constitution. At primary level, the child is very young and he may not be in a position to understand the various items in Fundamental Duties stated under Article 51A.

However, the first one to abide by the Constitution and respect its ideals and the National Flag and the National Anthem is important. Children should be made aware of the country's status and also its two important symbols, i.e. the National Flag and the National Anthem.

## NATIONAL IDENTITY

Besides the Constitution, National Flag and the National Anthem are the symbols of our unity. A citizen worthy of his name is expected to show due respect to the Flag. He should show similar respect to the National Anthem by standing up when it is sung or played. It is our duty not only to respect these symbols but also to defend their honour whenever there is a threat because they are also symbols of National Sovereignty. Defending one's country and dying for it is a sacred and houourable duty. These ideas should be developed in the minds of young children at the elementary level.

"When the National Anthem is played, everyone should stand up and should not move even an inch.

One should know the meaning of National Anthem and should be able to sing correctly. Children should be able to sing in group without any mistake and should be able to sing in tune".

Similar respect should be shown to the National Flag. Children should know the sequence of colour of the Indian Flag, i.e. orange at the top, white in the center and green at the bottom. On several occasions, it has been seen that the Flag is hoisted upside down. Similarly, the National Flag is always to be hoisted in the day time only and not at night. It should neither be spread on the floor nor a torn flag be hoisted.

Each individual is expected to be governed by the values and ideals given in our Constitution. At the school level a teacher is expected to develop awareness among the children about the preamble and the national level institutions, the National Flag and the National Anthem. In the morning assembly, the recitation of National Anthem should be compulsory on each day.

NPE 1986 visualised the national system of education based on National Curriculum Framework which contains a common core alongwith other components that are flexible. The common core will include the history of India's freedom struggle and other contents essential to nurture national identity.

It should be the duty of every citizen to cherish and follow the noble ideals which inspired our national struggle for freedom. It should be the duty of the teacher to identify the person or persons who participated in the freedom struggle and discuss the event with the students to develop a sense of pride among them.

## Identification of Values at Elementary School level

Following values have been identified for promotion at the elementary level, particularly keeping in view the age group of children and their understanding of the values together with the suggestive activities:

| | *Values* | | *Activities* |
|---|---|---|---|
| 1. | Cleanliness Hygiene | 1. | Checking the personal cleanliness of the student from time to time |
| 2. | Respect to parents, teachers and elders | 2. | Involving the children in cleaning the classroom and the surroundings |
| 3. | Truthfulness | 3. | Encouraging good eating habits in school and at Home |
| | | (i) | When a teacher enters the class, the children must stand and greet the teacher |
| | | (ii) | Standing at place while talking to the elders and telling stories about the necessity of truthfulness |

| | *Values* | | *Activities* |
|---|---|---|---|
| 4. | Obedience | 4. | Observing the students in or outside the class-room |
| 5. | Inquisitiveness | 5. | Encouraging the children to do simple experiments |
| | | (i) | Allowing them to observe things and draw conclusions |
| 6. | Punctuality | 6. | Encourage punctuality |
| 7. | Consideration and helpful Attitude towards others | 7. | Service to others and God |
| 8. | Self-help | 8. | Realization of the pleasure achieved when one helps others through role playing |
| 9. | Self-Confidence | 9. | Training them for assembly programme, CCA Programmes, academic competition, games, sports, etc. |
| 10. | Leadership | 10 | Giving responsibilities like maintaining discipline, games etc. |
| | | (i) | Making the children participate in group singing, discussions, etc. |
| | | (ii) | Telling the stories of national leaders |

As a child grows and reaches Class IV or V we may acquaint him with the life and works of great leaders who inspired our freedom as defined under Article 51A (IV). Similarly, a child must be made aware of the environment surrounding him. A child must be made to understand all the important areas of environment, like:

- Awareness of environment

- Protection of environment
- Preservation of environment

It shall be the duty of every citizen of India to protect and improve the National Environment including forests, lakes, wild life and to have compassion for living creatures. It was envisaged in the basic education that a school needs to have a garden. The children are expected to familiarise themselves with the process of growing of the plants. In the national curriculum framework for elementary education, environmental studies are a part of the school education curriculum. Therefore, the children get a good amount of knowledge about the environment.

A teacher has to ensure that children develop a habit of protecting the environment. For example, under the normal circumstances a child should not pluck leaves of plants. Perhaps visits to Gardens, Zoo or wild Life Parks would be very useful. Can we identify the values hidden in the Fundamental Duties. We need to compare Fundamental Duties and core component of national curriculum of elementary education.

**Inculcation of Values**

In the school equal respect is to be provided to both – a male and a female child. Display of anger or loss of temper should be avoided in the class-room. Needless to say that the biases reflected in the curriculum and textbooks are to be removed on priority basis. Wherever possible the examples of women are quoted in our books alongwith men. The traditional roles of women are to be shared with the men.

Following additional five steps have been identified for inculcation of values through school programme:

**1. Knowing :** The child must be made aware of the values through activities/programmes.

**2. Believing:** The child must develop faith in those values.

**3. Making Judgment:** The child must be provided conflicting situations to judge the implications of related values.

**4. Action:** The child may be encouraged to practise these values in actual life situations.

**5. Spontaneous:** Various programmes of schoolsmust take the child to that stage of action where the practice of values may become spontaneous.

## Value Education through Curricular Activities

Values could be promoted through direct or indirect methods. In the direct methods we may use related material in the class room and other activities like prayers, songs and stories etc. This could be achieved by direct methods. Values in the class-room should be linked up with the subjects like language, social sciences or natural sciences etc. Sometimes it is seen that students don't like a particular language and it is for the teacher to ensure that he makes it interesting by storytelling, signing or creating a situation interesting and joyful. Similarly, in social sciences the teacher should promote values and ideals of humanism, secularism, socialism and democracy. While teaching science subjects, developing scientific attitude is the main aim and varieties of human values can also be developed simultaneously.

In the indirect method, values could be promoted incidentally through staging drama, music, etc. A child may find strange that the values learnt at school, whether by direct or indirect method, are sometimes violated by elders at home. This may create a bad impression on the mind of the child which can be cleared by the teacher only.

## Value Education Through Co-curricular Activities.

The basic aim of fostering values among children is to get self-confidence, self-satisfaction and self-realisation. This can be adopted through morning assembly, discussions and through debates etc.

The values could be promoted by integrating school programmes with co-curricular and other such activities of the school like as ones given below:

**Morning Assembly :** It leads to punctuality, conducting orderly assembly, maintaining silence through meditation and Yoga.

**Prayer :** It gives peace of mind and self meditation.

**Programmes :** It may include pledge of loyalty to the nation, thought for the day, rationality and peace, storytelling, group songs, etc.

**Cultural Activities :** Group songs, folk dance, shadow play, one act play, fancy dress, etc.

**Games/Sports :** Celebrating Republic Day, Dussehra, Christmas Day, etc.

**Minimum Programme of Action for the School**

At the beginning of the academic year, the teacher may be given an orientation of the aims and objectives of value education.

*Morning Assembly*

It should include prayer, talks by teachers, patriotic songs, etc.

*Participation in Cultural Activities*

May comprise dance, drama, music, etc.

*Social service camps*

It includes visits and excursions to relevant places.

*Games, sports-meets at school*

The school must aim at good health for the children. Preparing human bodies for regional and national level competitions. The school must organise meets of various nature to imbibe different kinds of values in them. School should celebrate National Days, Annual Festivals, etc.

*Exhibitions*

On the history of freedom movement should be held in the school.

*Craft activities*

Should be arranged for the young children.

*Pictures and charts*

With short biographical notes on great men of the country should be putup in the class rooms and in the corridors.

Article 51A (e) relates to promoting harmony and the spirit of common brotherhood amongst all the people of India transcending religious, linguistic and regional or sectional diversities, to renouncing practices derogatory to the dignity of women.

Article 51A (f) relates to valuing and preserving the rich heritage of our composite culture...

These two clauses are closely related to the basic principles and ideals enshrined in the Constitution expressed in the Preamble as well as in other parts of the Constitution, particularly fundamental Rights, and to the characteristic features of Indian culture marked by variety and diversity of Indian nationhood. These clauses require that the school curriculum should help promote :

(a) an understanding that the people of India are composed of many diverse ethnic, cultural, religious and linguistic groups;

(b) an appreciation of this diversity as the essential condition for promoting harmony and the spirit of common brotherhood amongst all the people of India;

(c) knowledge of the status of women in Indian society and the understanding that every practice which is derogatory to the dignity of women and is repugnant to any civilised society is to be rejected;

(d) the knowledge understanding and appreciation of the composite nature of Indian culture, and

(e) an understanding of that view which seeks to attribute a rigid monolithic uniformity to Indian culture or present Indian culture as something static or the exclusive creation of any particular region, community or period of history are inimical to the objective of promoting harmony and the spirit of common brotherhood amongst all the people of India.

In teaching Social Science at Primary school level the curriculum and textbooks should introduce pupils to the way of living, religious beliefs, cultural patterns and customs of the people of India in different parts of the country. The main objective of teaching at this level of education is to enable the pupils appreciate cultural and ethnic similarities and differences and develop norms and behavior consistent with values like respect for others, different religions and ways of life and concern for others.

The pupils should understand rich cultural heritage which is essentially the result of the mixture of many groups.

### Values in the Class Room

Looking to the class room situation, it is essential to develop following values under the guidance of a teacher who is a role model:

***Good manners :*** Amicable settlement of disputes and polite interaction. Identifying lessons connected with these values, reading discussion. Role play or dramatisation of such incidents.

***Sharing :*** Children should be encouraged to share their books, notebooks; to help their class fellows in class work/ homework; to donate books and toys for handicapped and deprived children.

***Helpfulness :*** Famous quotations and lives of great men may be highlighted.

***Co-operation :*** Emphasis should be on building up patience and tolerance. Learning to get along with everyone in class, i.e. making new friends.

***Caring for pets and plants :*** Reading stories, rhymes, poems on animals and plants, especially on loyalty of pets.

***Punctuality :*** Discussion of lessons highlighting these values thus creating an awareness.

***Cleanliness :*** Laying emphasis on personal cleanliness, uniform, general hygiene (body parts). Keeping the class-room in order, neat and tidy.

## Role of Teachers

As members of the teaching community they themselves promote harmony and brotherhood. The teachers at the elementary level always reflect in their behaviour the spirit of common brotherhood.

In the class-room also a teacher is expected to promote harmony and the spirit of common brotherhood among the students.

It is noteworthy that the role of teachers during the next decades will be very important not only in the context of providing the dimension of values in our system of education but also in the context of providing more effective methods of education. Passage of time has not altered the moral of the story and rather the teacher's role has been made indispensible. He should necessarily be not only a good educator but a good person possessing basic moral aesthetic values. The teacher's influence is not confined to what he teaches in the class-room, in reality he teaches all the time. He is constantly watched by thousands of eyes; the way he walks and talks; conducts himself inside and outside the class-room; the company he keeps; his habits of thinking and studying; the way he treats his family and colleagues and all that he does is watched. Teacher lives in a glass house; he has hardly any private life. The teacher thus provides models–good or bad–of behaviour for his pupils.

# 2

# Secondary Education

*N.K. Ambasht* and *Sutpa Das*

India's history is an epitome of human values which enjoined on the society certain duties as a pre-condition of rights. Not only did it prescribe a set of duties for the different segments of the society but also during the period of education, these duties were internalised as a natural behaviour pattern.

Unfortunately, with the passage of time the entire education system has become predominantly concerned with 'information transmission' and the deliberate behaviour modification process started taking a back seat.

In the modern democratic society a set of duties become intrinsic to the sustenance of such a society. In fact these duties become a natural behaviour pattern of the individual and thereby of the entire citizenry. Today's child is the future citizen of the country. It is imperative to instill in the child certain duties as a pre-condition of rights. The child needs to grow into a better citizen with the firm understanding that right without obligations and obligation without rights give rise to slavery. Therefore, it is essential to be conscious of both rights as well as duties. In order to achieve this end, it become imperative that our institutions which nurture the future generations, namely the schools, should have these as a deliberate input in their scheme of things so as to train the future generations in democratic society, as responsible citizens. The role of schools has also been receding in this context with the onslaught of various media and information technology and yet they still remain the most potent source, for such an input.

Behaviour patterns as set of internalised stimulus response behaviour are the ultimate manifestations of duties. Schools have been trying, though with limited success, to inculcate the duties into the personal behaviour of its pupils through curricular instructions and processes. Duties are also intrinsically intertwind with values and go together. The adoption of the National Policy on Education (NPE), 1986 by the Parliament was a major landmark in this respect. It identified the components of the 'common core' which may be said to be providing the basic value framework and orientation of school curriculum in India. The National Policy which was adopted ten years after the incorporation of Fundamental Duties in the Constitution of India reflected almost each and every element mentioned in the Fundamental Duties.

'The common core', the NPE 1986 stated, 'will include the history of India's freedom movement, the constitutional obligations and other contents essential to nurture national identity. The Policy further laid down the following components of the 'common core': 'These elements will cut across subject areas and will be designed to promote values such as India's common cultural heritage, egalitarianism, democracy and secularism, equality of the sexes, protection of the environment, removal of social barriers, observance of the small family norm and inculcation of the scientific temper. All education programmes will be carried on in strict conformity with secular values'.

The present school curriculum has taken care to incorporate the 'common core' in the syllabus. To be more precise, the school curriculum has integrated duties connected with values of Independence, Constitutional

Obligation, Unity in Diversity, Composite Culture of India, Equality, Democracy, Gender Equality, Conservation of Environment, Small Family Norms, Scientific Temper, etc.

The Constitution of India under Article 51A has enumerated Fundamental Duties in the following manner:

Article 51A. It shall be the duty of every citizen of India:

(a) [to abide by the Constitution and respect its ideals and institutions, the National Flag and the National Anthem;

(b) to cherish and follow the noble ideals which inspired our national struggle for freedom;

(c) to uphold and protect the sovereignty unity and integrity of India;

(d) to defend the country and render national service when called upon to do so;

(e) to promote harmony and the spirit of common brotherhood amongst all the people of India transcending religious, linguistic and regional or sectional diversities: to renounce practices derogatory to the dignity of women;

(f) to value and preserve the rich heritage of our composite culture;

(g) to protect and improve the national environment including forests, lakes, rivers, wild life and to have compassion for living creatures;

(h) to develop the scientific temper, humanism and spirit of inquiry and reform;

(i) to safeguard public property and to abjure violence;

(j) to strive towards excellence in all the spheres of individual and collective activity two activity so that the nation constantly rises to higher levels of endeavour and achievement]

(k) who is a parent or guardian to provide opportunities for education to his child or, as the case may be, ward between the age of six and fourteen years] —(Added by the Constitution (Eighty-Sixth Amendment) Act, 2002 w.e.f. 1.4.2010).

It will be seen that almost all educable duties are incorporated in the school curriculum. At the same time it will be also seen that the Fundamental Duties include such items of behaviour which are to be made innate into the personality of the citizens and in many cases it cannot be enforced by law. For instance, if one does not develop scientific temper, or cherish and follow the 'noble ideals which inspired our national struggle for freedom', one cannot be sued in the court of law for not doing ones enjoined upon Fundamental Duty. How should it be decided as to what were the noble ideals? And how would one prove that one does or does not cherish these? Here it becomes important that education as a system in general, schools in particular, have such activities/ programmes that the expected pattern of behaviour gets ingrained into the individual citizens and becomes a natural part of the personality.

A basic question that can be asked is, 'Are our schools with all the text-books and curricular materials producing such citizens?' The answer is obviously a big NO. Then what interventions are required to be made?

One might like to attempt an answer on two scores. One, what kind of modifications can be made in the curriculum, particularly in the transactional process' to make already existing curricular materials more effective so as to maximize the internalisation of learning into the innate behaviour pattern of the learner, and what shall be the procedure of assessing evaluating? Is our examination system so designed as to make an assessment of such abstract personality traits? If not, what modification and weightage is required to be given to these aspects of personal behaviour including adherence to Fundamental Duties?

Two, emanating from these questions is related as to what kind of teacher preparation programmes should be enforced to build the capacity of the teacher to be able to transact these programmes in the school as to achieve the ends as envisaged and as is imperative of the Fundamental Duties. The teacher's role is important. His/her imagination and preparation, leadership and encouragement, the insight into the needs and limitations of the pupils, and the teachers's thorough knowledge of the community alone can take teaching from the class-room and the text-books out into the midst of the community making it a real laboratory of learning. Such commitments can only measure the success of teacher preparation programmes.

The teacher has to guide/motivate the students to carry out meaningful activities and projects. A few samples of activities as listed below may help the teacher to reach the desired goal.

**Activities / Projects**

(i) Students may discuss and adopt the constitution of the Students Council as they study the Indian Constitution;

(ii) The voting procedure and election rules may be studied during the time of any local election in collaboration with election officials;

(iii) Through class-room discussions the teacher may try to encourage his / her students to take a responsible stand on current issues and problems like environmental pollution, etc.

(iv) The students may be helped to organize blood donation camps, fund raising camps or any similar kind of national service in times of war, aggression or war like situation;

(v) Wherever possible the students themselves may organise certain porgrammes like assembly, social gatherings and athletic meets in their schools;

(vi) Students may be asked to plan a programme to improve thier behaviour in reading rooms/ library, canteen, assembly, etc.;

(vii) Students may be encouraged to invite freedom fighters, if any, in the city or in the village nearby, and organize a discussion about India's freedom struggle;

(viii) Since historical monuments are rare and irreplaceable part of the national heritage, the students may be encouraged to chalk out a programme to maintain and preserve historical monuments nearby;

(ix) Students may be encouraged to focus the attention of people and authorities of their locality on any steps to be taken to improve the services in their school or outside;

(x) Films such as Haqqikat, Gandhi, Sardar may be shown to students and discussions held;

(xi) The Students may be asked to prepare a list of public buildings and monuments of their locality or town and locate them on a sketch map.

(xii) The students may be encouraged to prepare a short questionnaire and conduct opinion poll to ascertain the views of local people on the performance of the democratic bodies at the grass root level i.e., the local bodies of their place;

(xiii) In order to develop a scientific outlook, the teachers should :

(a) discuss the influence of physical conditions on food, dress, customs, art and architecture,

(b) encourage students to collect conflicting reports on an issue and look for the truth.

(xiv) There is a need for a fundamental transformation in the direction and approach to the curricula for teaching Fundamental Duties in schools and teacher education institutions. Citizenship values should be understood by all concerned as combination of rights and duties. Appropriate steps in this regard need to be initiated through the educational process to achieve the desired results in the long run;

(xv) Creating more awareness of the Fundamental Duties in citizens through advocacy and sensitisation programmes is the prime need of the time. The Preamble to the Constitution of India and the 10 (now 11) clauses of Article 51A relating to Fundamental Duties could be appropriately displayed on all government publications, diaries, calendars, and at public places, etc. so that they always remain in the focus of the citizens. This should be done in all Indian languages in the States/UTs;

(xvi) Preamble to the Constitution of India and eleven clauses of Article 51A of the Constitution regarding Fundamental Duties be printed, in all the school text-books, supplementary materials and general publications brought out by the NCERT, (Instructions to this effect have already been issued by the NCERT). The State Governments will now be requested for a similar action on schools text-books brought out by States;

(xvii) The intent of each clause of Article 51A could be a subject of brief presentation in all morning assemblies in the schools, and the teacher education institution in by the Heads of the Institutions or some senior members of the staff, highlighting the need of internalizing the values inherent in the Fundamental Duties. Such presentation could continue throughout the academic session covering all aspects underlying the clauses;

(xviii) Seminars, debates, competitions on different aspects of Article 51A could be made a regular feature of the co-curricular programmes of the schools, colleges and universities;

(xix) A sensitisation module based on Fundamental Duties be made an integral part of all in-service teacher education programmes by national, state and district level institutions. Fundamental Duties could be included in the Foundation Course in Teacher Education Curriculum;

(xx) Development of radio and video spots highlighting important messages emanating from the clauses of article 51A, in the background of proper music and national flag to transmit in all regional languages by All India Radio, Doordarashan and other DD channels through the involvement of such media persons as are known for innovative presentation of nationally important messages;

(xxi) January 3 (the date on which Article 51A came into force) be observed as Fundamental Duties Day.

# 3

# Citizenship Development and Higher Education

***R.B. Jain***

Citizenship is the lifeline of a civilised society. It is central to the socio-economic development of the individual, society and nation. But what is meant by citizenship? What are the elements of good citizenship, and how can the good be achieved? It is really very difficult to answer these questions because the concept of citizenship varies with the cultural background and the stages of economic and social development of the society. However, there are certain elements, which are common to good citizenship in all circumstances: obligation, responsibility and duty. A good citizen should not merely treat the state as an institution from which he derives rights, but also as one to which a citizen has corresponding duties. In this paper, it is attempted to understand the concept of good citizenship and the values underlying the concept, with the objective of suggesting some practical steps to enforce it in the realm of higher education in India. But it would not be out of place first to understand the concept of citizenship.

## Concept of Citizenship

The roots of the concept of citizenship may be traced to the days of the ancient city-state of Athens. During those days, the inhabitants of Athens were divided into two categories – citizens and slaves. While citizens enjoyed all rights; civil and political, the slaves had no rights. These rights enabled the Athenian citizens to take an effective share in the government of the state. The situation was not very different in ancient Rome or in the European medieval free cities – except that in medieval Europe, place of slaves was taken by the serfs. It was only after the French Revolution that the conception of citizenship was gradually broadened to include all the indigenous adult population of the state. Today, most of the societies are modern democracies in the sense that they are based on the principle of the right of the citizens to elect their government. Though, owing to the large size of the state it is not possible for each and every individual to participate directly in the functioning of the government, there is an indirect participation.

The conception of citizenship has been broadening with the passage of time and onward march of democracy. In Ancient Greece and Rome and in medieval times, a citizen was an inhabitant of a city, who enjoyed its 'freedom' or was admitted to its special privileges. The number of these citizens was invariably much smaller than those of non-citizen residents – slaves, serfs, and others who were without leisure, and all members of the fair sex were excluded from the category of citizens. In modern times a citizen is a member of state who possesses 'Rights which are regarded by society as necessary for his development, except for a small number of aliens, insane and morally depraved persons or criminals who may have some limitations as to the quantum of their rights. Humanity has advanced to the extent of having a Universal Declaration of Human Rights adopted by the General Assembly of the United Nations on 10 December, 1948. Thus the possession of 'Rights' has been regarded as an essential characteristics of citizenship in all ages and climes.

The concept of citizenship today has become more

positive, constructive and comprehensive. The concept presupposes the possession of full political rights by the individual. In other words, a citizen is a person who possesses not only civil rights such as the right to life, personal freedom, property, contract, etc., but also political rights e.g. the right to vote, contest elections. This requires that the citizens who possess full rights also owe several obligations, responsibilities and duties, towards the state and the society at large. A citizen owes allegiance and loyalty to the state and may be called upon to sacrifice even his life to protect and preserve the sovereignty of his nation. The long-term growth and development of the society demands the present generation of citizens to make sacrifices to enable the future generation to live in peace and plenty. Citizenship, therefore, is not a mere passive possession of certain rights, but also an active participation in the life of the community with a view to self-realisation and consciously promoting social good. A good citizen is excepted to play a more significant and meaningful role in the society.

Laski, an eminent political scientist, has opined that rights are correlative with functions. 'I have them that I may make my contribution to the social end– I have no claim to receive without the attempt, at least, to pay for what I receive – whatever form any payment takes, it is essential that I should realize that the Rights I have are given to me because I am performing some given duties.' Rights are not outside the society but inherent in it. Their conferment by the state on the individual is aimed at development and progress not only of the individual but also of the society. Article 29(1) of the Declaration of Universal Rights provides, 'Every one has duties to community in which alone the free and full development of his personality is possible.' Hence, every right carries with it corresponding duty and all rights must be exercised in a manner so as to promote the general social well being.

There is thus a three-fold relationship between Rights and Duties. Firstly, the very fact that the Rights are conferred on the individual by the Sate or the Constitution casts upon the individual the duty that they are exercised in a manner so as to promote the social good. Secondly, the Rights conferred on the individual can become effective only if they are recognised and respected by the other members of the community, they cast upon the individual the duty of recognizing and respecting the Rights of others. Thirdly, every right carries with it a corresponding duty, e.g. the right of vote carries with it the duty to vote, i.e. he must perform the primary duty of a citizen in democracy to see that he helps to elect suitable individuals as his governors, and that he carries out his duty of keeping strict vigilance over the actual executives. In nutshell, it would not be an exaggeration to say that the successful working of democracy is not possible unless the citizens discharge their duties with a sense of responsibility, intelligence and diligence.

Broadly speaking, there can be two categories of duties-legal and moral. Legal duties are those which are capable of being enforced through the courts of law while moral duties are carried out either out of fear of public opposition or any other moral reasons. Education for citizenship has for its main objective the rousing of consciousness in the hearts of the people that performance of public duties and social service are essential both for individual and social good and the progress of humanity. In this matter of the enforcement of duties, legal sanctions play a very insignificant role the rise of social consciousness, the imbibing of the public spirit and the creation of responsive environment and proper atmosphere are of greater importance. Among the duties that a citizen is excpected to perform are: allegiance to the state, the obligation of obedience, the duty to pay various taxes, the duty to assist government in the maintenance of law and order and other social welfare schemes, the duty to vote and to exercise vigilance, and several civic duties, without which the creation of a peaceful, welfare-oriented, harmonious society is not possible.

**Good Citizenship and the Indian Constitution**

The key to the concept of good citizenship is the concept of democracy and its underlying assumptions – equality, liberty and fraternity.

The concept of good citizenship is closely related to the concept of duty. Every citizen should understand that he should not bother himself whether others are doing their duty but he should carry out his own duties. The emergence of free India gave us the privileges of good citizenship. However, our independence as citizens has not been fortified and enriched by a collective sense of responsibility. Because of this lack of duty-consciousness, we have in our society, evils and malpractices like misbehavior, indiscipline, lawbreaking – all these leading to the weakening of the state and society. The only way to eschew these and other social evils is to enforce and respect the fundamental duties that a citizen owes to the state and fellow beings and that are now part of our constitutional obligations. Another pre-condition of good citizenship is the will and capacity to struggle against and overcome obstacles and foster a healthy environment, physical and social, in which man can rise to the highest social excellence and enjoy the fruits of culture and civilisation.

The only way to the achievement of citizenship development is by identifying the hardcore of citizenship values enshrined in the Constitution and making a concerted effort to protect and promote them. The values that emerge from the provisions of the Constitution are:

(i) Many problems in human relations have their source in the desire of one person to dominate over others;

(ii) Every citizen must accept the equality of all citizens;

(iii) All citizens enjoy the basic freedoms and human rights and must provide the same to each other;

(iv) Democracy demands respect for dissent and opposite views;

(v) Change can be brought about by peaceful means and responsible behaviour towards fellow citizens;

(vi) The highest functionaries of state are first the citizens and therefore, responsible to their fellow citizens and their well-being;

(vii) Self-discipline and responsibilities to fellow citizens are important;

(viii) Right to vote provides to every adult an opportunity to participate in the political process;

(ix) Constant vigilance over the conduct of functionaries ministries, members, administrators etc. is the price citizens must pay;

(x) Dignity of individual is important with every citizen respecting and protecting the individual dignity of every other citizen.

Citizenship is an important duty, which every individual must discharge with responsibility and dedication. A responsible and vigilant citizenry can play a vital role in strengthening of democracy by sensitizing the administration to the needs of the people and ensuring accountability of the executive authority.

Peace, harmony and tolerance are other pre-requisites of good citizenship. We should inculcate and accept the basic values of peace and harmony and learn to be tolerant in our minds.

The Constitution of India, while guaranteeing fundamental rights to Indian citizens and others, also lays down the duties of the country's citizens. Article 51A of the Constitution, inserted in 1976 enumerates these duties. This article provides that it shall be the duty of every citizen of

India – to abide by the Constitution and respect its ideals and institutions, the National Flag and the National Anthem; to cherish and follow the noble ideals which inspired our national struggle for freedom; to uphold and protect the sovereignty, unity and integrity of India; to defend the country and render national service when called upon to do so; to promote harmony and the spirit of common brotherhood amongst all the people of India transcending religious, linguistic and regional or sectional diversities, to renounce practices derogatory to the dignity of women; to value and preserve the rich heritage of our composite culture; to protect and improve the natural environment including forests, lakes, rivers and wild life and to have compassion for living creatures; to develop the scientific temper, humanism and the spirit of inquiry and reform; to safeguard public property and to abjure violence; to strive towards excellence in all spheres of individual and collective activity so that the nation constantly rises to the highest levels of endeavour and achievement; and to provide opportunities for education to our children or wards, between the age of six and fourteen years.

## Good Citizenship and Higher Education

University students constitute one of the most knowledgeable, dynamic and progressive components of the society. The question that the present paper seeks to examine is as to how the concept of citizenship development be enforced in the realm of higher education in India. The above analysis of the concept of good citizenship clearly establishes that the concept underlines such values as tolerance, responsibility, duty and obligations. Hence the specific question that arises is how to enforce fundamental duties and inculcate the spirit of adherence to state in the citizens' rights from their birth to the elementary, middle and secondary education and right through the higher educational institutions. However, this paper has a limited objective to discuss some specific measures to activise the value of good citizenship in the realm of higher education, before suggesting some practical measures to enhance the understanding and practice of fundamental duties and citizenship values in higher education. Let us first identify some of the features of university system pointing to the realities of the higher educational system in India.

**Universities in India**

University studentship is a transitory phase of life that lasts normally for minimum three to five years (however, the period is longer in case someone decides to pursue post-graduate studies). This phase of life is, on the one hand bidding good-bye to days of adolescence and on the other welcoming the adulthood. In other words, the life in this phase in sandwiched between needs of last stage of adolescence and burden of adulthood. The individuals are biologically adult, but socially irresponsible and idealistic. They tend to judge this world in extreme terms–right or wrong, good or bad and just or unjust. Max Weber once observed that youth has a tendency to follow "a pure picture of absolute ends: while maturity is associated with an ethic of responsibility". Max Weber's views may appear exaggerated at the first stance, it is, however, true that the youth has the tendency to be more and more idealistic than pragmatic and responsible. They tend to see the world in terms of what it should be instead of what it is. They are more likely to offer all encompassing solutions to social problems than their elders. The bases of a good society in their viewpoint are such values as freedom, equality, efficiency, and justice as social welfare.

The youth in university is characterised by relative freedom from familial control and responsibilities – financial and others which makes college life an exciting experience for many students. Society treats them with leniency, indulgence and liberality.

Most of the students, as long as they are in the university, are without any part time employment and lack independent source of income. They depend on their parents or educational institutions (in some cases) for financial support. Psychologically this period is one of stress and change, which has an important bearing on the attitudes and orientations of the students.

The youth feels the need of autonomy during this period of life and has a tendency to rebel against authority– parental, educational and social – which is quite great. College and university students also live under various kinds of stresses, anxieties and strains, which upset their mental equilibrium, many students by virtue of modern education and western culture, feel alienated from the traditional pattern of society. There is much wavering in the student community.

The demands of academic life and more particularly the pressure of examination leave little time to students for extra-curricular activities. Serious students regard studentship as a period of preparation for entry into the uncertain world of employment. The lowermiddle class with rural background in case of majority of students and lack of security contribute to their gradual alienation from academic ethics. The corruption, inefficiency and apathy of governmental actions also precipitate their opposition to the established regime.

An important feature of university studentship is growing students' activism in politics. Student activism has taken a variety of forms – agitation and movements and support of one major party or the other. Students take part in both on-campus and off-campus politics. It gives the students the experience of elections, which is a key component of democratic process. At the same time students are also the targets of exploitation by vested political interests. Various types of cultural recreational professional associations and the college unions are instrumental in furnishing a wide range of opportunities for undertaking constructive and well organised programmes and shoulder responsibilities as citizens.

Another harsh reality of the educational system is that there is no homogeneity among the students' community. In fact, some sort of homogeneity and unity did exist among the students in an earlier era when higher education was elitist in orientation and it was open only for the members of rich and elite families. But, increasingly open and mass educational system that prevails in India today tends to recruit students from all sections of the society, and hence generates heterogeneity amongst students' community comprising of varying individual traits and objectives. If on the one hand we have students' who are very much dedicated to college and its activities, there are others who are completely indifferent to it, then there are those who favour student movements of an exclusively academic type or take part in active political movements. In other words, there are carrier minded students who are academically oriented and politically activist students who are apolitical and academically also average. The number of students and institutions should be regulated.

University students seem to be lost and confused because they are unable to see any relevance between what they learn on the campus and what they observe in the society. Because of this the task of the leaders has become especially onerous. There is an urgent need for communication between the teachers, students and the administrators of the educational institutions who present the target groups in the higher education system. It is essential that not only newer approaches to and innovative methods of teaching to make the field of inquiry more interesting for the students be employed but efforts should be made to reduce the communication gap between these targets to secure more harmonious relationship between them and an understanding of each other's duties as citizens.

In a nutshell, one can say that a study of higher educational institutions in India in modern times presents quite a disturbing and disappointing picture. The biggest evils that plague them at present are the lack of commitment to any value system at all and prevalence of indiscipline, violence, student unrest, show of money power and display of arrogance and hollow and fast life. In order to reform the existing situation, there is an urgent need for inculcating some moral values and duties and obligations of a citizen amongst the three target groups in the college education – the students, teachers and administrators. It is in this context that we present below some concrete, general and specific suggestions to inculcate the concept of fundamental duties in the field of higher education.

### Activizing Citizenship Values

We should now consider some of the practical steps that could be undertaken for inculcating the citizenship duties at the higher levels of education. As already indicated there are three target groups that need to be addressed in this respect – the students, the teachers and the management and administrative personnel. We shall take up the consideration of activities to be undertaken for each of these groups in the same order.

### The Students

The students are the primary target group at the higher educational level. It is important that their orientation towards these citizenship duties be made from the very beginning of their college life as soon as they enter the portals of the college or the university. For this purpose, it is suggested that a compulsory orientation training programme in the awareness of what constitutes citizenship duties be given to all the entrants as a part of their co-curricular activities immediately after they join the university/ college. The orientation programme may be based on the syllabus developed by the University of Bombay on Citizenship Development. Now that UGC has developed a number of core courses relating to Article 51A such as foundation courses and core courses in applied components at the under graduate level, it is desirable that the colleges and the universities should be able to implement these courses as a part of their orientation programmes towards imparting to the students awareness of their duties. This orientation is important for all entrants to higher education and for students of any stream in science, social science, technology, or professional courses. And these programmes should be repeated every year, at least at the under graduate levels.

It has been observed that in many colleges and universities provisions exist regarding composition of different types of associations for students' co-curricular activities. However, many of these provisions remain in abeyance because of many obstacles, financial or otherwise, and the student's community does not get to form these associations. It is of utmost importance that the students be encouraged to form associations at different levels : subject, sports, recreational, cultural and voluntary associations for self-help or community services. These associations or organisations will help the inculcation of the feeling of one's obligations towards each other and towards the college/university/institution to which they belong and also towards the community. In this way they will have the urge in a practical way to inculcate these obligatory duties into their behavioural pattern. The process of electing and forming committees and entering into discussion will inculcate in them the habit of respect for the point of view of others, and arriving at decisions through a process of collective discussion and consensus. In many institutions, there is a provision of student activities through N.S.S. and N.C.C. These two organisations are very important in inculcating a sense of self-discipline and awareness of community problems and help solving these problems. Most of the activities of the students incorporating their responsibilities towards the community at large get operationalised through these two organisations, and at the end of the students' stay in the college, the authorities can give them certificates indicating that they have been very active in the community work.

At the time of the formulation of unions and conducting elections, it is important that there is an input from the side of the teachers in as much as the teachers incharge of such activities owe an obligation to the students to make them aware of their duties and responsibilities in conducting the affairs of the student unions in a peaceful and harmonizing manner more so at the time of elections – to observe discipline and code of conduct and not to abuse freedom of expression or use any violent methods. It is at this time that the duties enshrined in the Constitution get their greatest manifestation in practical terms.

In most cultural / sports/recreational activities, the students should be encouraged to shoulder responsibilities for managing their own events and observing obligations which accrue to them as a result of their being in positions of responsibility.

It has been observed that both the students and the teachers use their unions for such practices which do not leave either to the students or the teachers opportunities to indulge in negative tactics such as prolonged strikes or demonstrations or continuing disruption in legitimate academic activity. These students have a basic duty to observe discipline and self-restraint for carrying on those activities which promote the cause of higher learning. The teachers have an equal duty not to indulge in trade unionism which results in prolonged disruptions in the academic activity. While trade unionism is a legitimate tool to some extent for many commercial trade unions, practising it in educational institutions does not in any way enhance the prestige of the teachers or the students.

**Obligations towards the Community**

At regular intervals during the period of their stay in the institutions, the students should be encouraged to organize activities relating to some of the most pressing issues facing the community. They should be encouraged to go out in the field, i.e. the nearby villages or communities where specific problems like the non-availability of certain services or problems arising out or certain natural or man-made calamities arise and solution for mitigating them should be found and implemented. This could be a regular exercise as a part of their extra-curricular activities.

Students should be encouraged to organize model parliaments in order to discuss certain specific issues facing the nation and to formulate possible solutions. The organisation of model/mock parliaments may also be directed towards specific problem of the observance of the rules and regulations for conducting the business of the House. The students can realize the importance of observing the basic rules of politics at the formative stage, and carry this early orientation to their later stage of life. In this connection, the Bureau of Parliamentary Research and Training in the Parliament Secretariat can tender some useful help and guidance to the students.

For developing the feeling of nationalism and integrity in respect of the nation's symbols and institutions it is necessary that on various national days, Gandhi's Birth Anniversary and other similar occasions, a series of lectures, symposia and workshops be organised to make the students aware of the importance of these occasions and make them meaningful. This should become regular feature of the activities of the educational institutions.

A number of Fundamental Duties enshrined in the Constitution like promotion of harmony and common brotherhood, transcending religious, linguistic and regional diversities should find their expression in the community living of students particularly in the hostels and group housing. Some of the activities already suggested above should also be operationalised in the premises of the hostels and similar other places.

Protection of environment has become a very crucial problem of mankind in the present century. The student community at the college level not only can have the spirit of responsibility for taking steps to promote the improvement of environment but can also be catalyst for spreading the message of the importance of environmental protection amongst the masses. The students should not only observe the environment day, but should also undertake specific steps to inculcate the feeling of responsibilities among the citizens towards this mammoth enterprise.

Finally, it is important that in the activities undertaken by student, emphasis should be on the aspects of community welfare at large. Students should be provided with such opportunities which prompt them to observe their Fundamental Duties enshrined in the Constitution.

## II. Activities including Citizenship

## Duties amongst the Teachers

Along with the students, it is important that teachers should also observe their duties towards their students as also towards the institution which they serve. The non-observance of the duties on the part of the teachers would encourage a sense of defiance on the part of the students. The teachers must be apprised of the fact that their first obligation is towards their students, for whom they exist. They should be told not to cut classes, to be punctual and regular in taking classes, and to observe certain moral code in the class-room, like being courteous and helpful to their students in their academic pursuits. Since they have the primary obligation towards their students, they owe a duty towards themselves to provide the students free access to them irrespective of any discrimination of any kind and to be available to them for consultation and guidance at certain reasonable hours which must be specified by them in advance at the beginning of the session.

Apart from the academic consultation, it is also important that the teachers act as an important source of encouragement and as guides towards their career building and counseling. They have the duty of counseling their students about the prospects for employment so that their anxiety about their future prospects is somewhat reduced.

At this stage of one's life, students also need counseling in respect of their stresses and strains due to the conditions of modern, competitive pattern of social living and due to extraneous factors of family or domestic concerns. Teachers have to assume some responsibility in relation to these situations for guiding and counseling students.

The teacher community constitutes an important catalyst towards character building of the students. The teachers owe a duty to take positive steps and guide the students through their own examples or other role models to help the students in building their responsibilities in their individual lives. This is a specific obligation which accrues to the teacher community and every teacher should draw satisfaction from the fact that he has been able to help the students in moulding their character.

## III. Duties of Management and Staff

It has been observed that the staff and management of the institution where the students spend major portion of their youth have no concern or awareness about the difficulties or inconveniences the students suffer on account of the perceived non-compliance of the rules and regulations of the university or institution on the part of the staff. It is important that the staff and management observe a two-way process of communication where the students be made aware about their continuing responsibilities of observing the various rules of rightful living and obligation as also the deadlines or regulations which they must strictly adhere to. Adequate use of Notice-boards, Circulars, College and University Newsletters or Announcements through the press for observing the concerned obligations is a must on the part of the staff and management. They should also establish certain complaints and grievances procedures and appeals from the decisions of the subordinate staff for redress of the genuine complaints and grievancs of the students. The management and staff must be ensured that students are in know of their continuing duties towards themselves, towards their institutions and towards the community at large. In addition, it is also important that the staff displays a sense of personal concern for their genuine difficulties at every level of their mutual interactions.

Finally, it is also necessary that in order to build-up the sense of partnership amongst the students, teachers and the management and staff, informal contacts through cultural associations or frequent get-togethers be encouraged. It would also be helpful if there are regular meetings between those three target groups to evolve a solution for their continuing common problems.

## Concluding Observations

The above suggestions made in the context of operationalisation of citizenship duties amongst the student community at the higher educational level are neither exhaustive nor conclusive enough to improve the existing situation. These represent only a beginning in the understanding of the value of citizenship development. It is important that the colleges and universities develop elaborate mechanisms for implementing these programmes relating to each of these groups and monitoring their progress from time to time with a view to stimulating awareness on their part of the importance of observing their respective citizenship duties and values. Not only such mechanisms need to be reviewed periodically but also put into active practice. As the above activities get operationalised many avenues would open themselves for further experimentation in the implementation of the process of citizenship development. This is an open-ended process and we must not close further options available in citizenship development as a result of the above activities.

# 4

# People's Representatives from Panchayat to Parliament

*J. Veeraraghavan*

As citizens of the country, the elected representatives have the same rights and duties as any others. But as leaders and exemplars, their responsibility is even greater in this regard. Further in Parliament and the legislatures, the elected representatives take a specific oath to adhere to and uphold the Constitution. They are, therefore, duty bound to uphold and propagate the observance of Fundamental Duties by one and all.

The 73rd and 74th amendments to the Constitution in 1992 have taken the form of democratic government to the district and village levels. These amendments have strengthened the three-tier system which had been advocated and practised with success in varying degrees in different parts of the country. Power is thus flowing to the grassroot levels and provision has also been made for reservation for women in addition to the reservation for Scheduled Castes and Scheduled Tribes in the elections at this level. The State governments have been asked by Article 243H to authorize panchyats to levy and collect appropriate taxes and similar provisions are made with reference to the functioning of municipal bodies. As the system of local governance gets further strengthered, the elected representatives have a major role in ensuring that Fundamental Duties become a living reality for our masses.

In today's context, the most important among the fundamental duties are those that are specified in Article 51A (e) and (f) namely, the duty:

> to promote harmony and the spirit of common brotherhood amongst all the people of India transcending religious, linguistic and regional and sectional diversities; to renounce practices derogatory to the dignity of women;
>
> to value and preserve the rich heritage of our composite culture.

These are also related powerfully to 51A (c) viz. the duty 'to uphold and protect the sovereignty, unity and integrity of India'.

Respect for all living things, especially for the weak and the elderly, moderation in all matters including goals related to pursuit of wealth, power and status, the observance of the eternal moral code of Dharma, tolerance of and positive regard for differing religions and ethos are some of the distinguishing characteristics of Indian culture. In this it differs from the Western or modern culture which over-emphasizes the aggressive acquisition of material comforts and encourages a high degree of individualism. The Indian culture does not disregard the need for material comforts and the development of individuality but these are always subordinated to social obligations and a cosmic view of life that seeks to reach the Immortal and the Permanent behind the ever changing world.

The use of caste, religion, language or other sectional interests for creating an emotional bias to help win in elections is contrary to Indian culture and to the Fundamental Duties. To create or provoke disputes based on religion, caste, etc. is a positive act of crime to be abhorred by all thinking men and especially by people's representatives who represent all the people and not a section of them. The elections constitute a great educational process and what is said and done during the election campaigns is of great importance. The candidates seeking the mandate of the people have to keep their obligations under the Fundamental Duties constantly in view while conducting their campaigns. In the later stages of the campaigns when emotions are aroused and there is much bitterness and hatred, it is all the more important for the candidates to keep their cool and restrain their supporters from saying or doing anything that could arouse caste, religion, language or other sectional emotions and fears. They should remember all the time that success achieved through improper and false propaganda is as much a corrupt practice as the use of money or muscle power.

For operationalising the duties inherent in the promotion of national unity and integrity and upholding the dignity of women and the integrity of the country, the elected representatives can contribute a great deal by positively encouraging all activities designed to promotes these values. They should make it a point to visit all educational and cultural institutions in their constituency and create a network of activities through them that promote solidarity and friendship among all the people and remove of all misgivings, fears, dislikes and factors that cause disunity. They should persuade the educational institutions to identify the positive and negative factors promoting or inhibiting national unity and dignity of women and help them promote positive factors. They can play a role in scotching rumour mongering and activities designed to provoke emotions and prejudices of sections of the community. They can do so before and after the elections and contribute significantly to unity and integrity of the nation.

Article 51A (b) enjoins the citizens to cherish and follow the noble ideals which inspired our national struggle for freedom. Our struggle for freedom was no mere fight to end the foreign rule. Our fight was also to get rid ourselves of age old poverty, unemployment, ignorance and superstition. That is why, Mahatma Gandhi emphasised "The Talisman". He said, when taking a decision, think of the poorest and see if it will benefit him, and that would be the talisman for taking decision. That is why Jawaharlal Nehru emphasised the need for modern science and technology and their application to solve people's problems, the need for dissolving superstitions and blind faith and opening up of people's minds through education. Resisting the inroads of Western rationality and materialism into our culture, in order to preserve our cosmic view of universe, is important. That, however, does not mean a regression into superstition. India, once in the vanguard of civilisation, went down in history when knowledge became petrified into dogmas. We cannot allow that to happen again. The legislators have a duty to promote science, technology and knowledge and their application to solve people's problems and fight against ignorance and superstition in all its forms. The role of educational institutions in this matter is obvious and it is the duty of elected representatives to encourage and assist educational institutions in playing this role.

Unemployment and poverty are foremost among the problems of the people. A representative of the people would be finally judged by his contribution to solving these problems. It is now recognised that these problems cannot be solved by mere foreign aid or government programmes. Funds from abroad and governments budgets are important but by themselves insufficient. While trying for a share in the national cake, it is important that people are taught to be self-reliant. The people must be provided opportunities for learning and education and for organising their productive skills in the service of their fellow men with honesty and integrity. Economic progress depends on honest and productive service and not in unproductive expenditure. If a legislator brings a school, a hospital, railway line or a factory to his constituency, he is to be applauded, provided he has adopted fair and reasonable means for the achievement, but he is to be applauded even more if he ensures that these institutions function effectively and fulfil their roles. If, for instance, he has founded a college and appoints all his cronies and castemen and supporters, in preference to more meritorious persons, he is the enemy of his people and not their friend. For, by providing bad education he destroys the future of countless young men and women and also sets an example of nepotism. No society and no economy can advance without recognition and support to merit and excellence. It is the duty of the elected representatives to educate the people on the importance of recognising merit and excellence and honest work at all levels.

As people's representative, he should ponder as to why India has been so unsuccessful in solving the problems of poverty and unemployment? Is it not because we have failed to provide opportunities to the young to develop their potential and to become self-reliant? Is it also because we have failed to take a strong stand against large families (increase in population) and against illiteracy (large dropouts from school)? Is it not the task of elected representatives to organize local opinion and resources for successfully controlling population growth and promote educational advance and growth of small and medium enterprises? Equality was a great ideal of the freedom movement. It continues to be so, even more today. While we all should work for greater equality and reduction is disparities, there would be little meaning in these concepts, if these do not lead to economic progress. Our commitment to equality should not be allowed to come in the way of economic progress or wealth generation. Elected representatives have many opportunities for educating the people on the importance of wealth generation and equality of opportunity, and the need to work for both these goals.

Non-interference in the functioning of governmental institutions (and non-governmental institutions) is essential for ensuring efficiency and equity. As representatives of the people, MLAs, MPs and District Panchayat representatives will receive many petitions and representations for redressal of grievances or for other purposes. It is their duty to take up the causes of those with genuine grievances and complaints but they should do so witout resort to "arm-twisting". They should indeed discourage favouring officials who seek to please them and instead insist on objectivity in their behaviour. Nowhere else is this more important that in relation to law enforcing agencies. Elected representatives must not only observe the laws in letter and in spirit and help law enforcing agencies in detecting law breakers and in punishing them. Much has been written in regard to criminalisation of politics. In so far as the very process of election is to facilitate the making and enforcing of laws, it is ironical that law makers should in public mind be identified with law breakers!!

The reason why elected representatives sometimes hinder law enforcement is their fear of losing the support of some of their followers indulging in unlawful activity. Also, there is, often, in the prevailing feudal atmosphere, the question of "status". A Member of Parliament occupying a railway berth reserved for another feels humiliated if asked to vacate the berth, for his "status" falls in the eyes of his supporters. In such instances, it is the duty of the elected representative to explain the law to his supporters and to educate them away from the false addiction to status which belongs to ancient times which are no more relevant.

Similarly, in taking his decisions the elected representative must be objective and not guided by any bias or prejudice. It is often said that no one is free from some bias. That is all the more reason for specifically examining the facts especially to see if there is any bias in one's actions or opinions.

Self-scrutiny and reflection thus become essential. Ultimately, the elected representative has to act according to his conscience, in the interest of the country and the interest of his constituency. If there is a conflict, the country's interest must override his constituency's and his conscience must override everything. Although on most occasions there will be no conflicts. In Premchand's story, Panch Parameshwar, we have the instance of the Panchyat Chairman who is to give a verdict in a case involving a rival with whom he has long standing enemity. He is looking forward to the day when with his verdict he can deal a mortal blow to his rival. But such is the power of conscience that when the time comes for verdict, conscience and objectivity prevail and the sacredness of the position of Panchayat Chairman prevails over everything else.

The concept of Dharma is firmly rooted in Indian tradition. Dharma is complex, but has to prevail. It means one has to do one's duty, one has to do what is right, but one must also understand what is right and what one's duty is. But once the Dharma is understood, one cannot flinch from it no matter what the consequences. Dharma therefore is the protector of society. Adherence to Dharma by every elected representative will lead to value based politics and lay the foundations of well being for the people. The Seven Principles of Public Life enumerated by the Lord Nolan Committee on Standards in Public Life submitted to Parliament in the United Kingdom give a modern and clear version of the Dharma of a legislator (as of other public functionaries) and are summarised below:

> They should take decisions solely in terms of the public interest and not in order to gain financial or other material benefits for themselves, their family, or their friends–(Selflessness).
>
> They should not place themselves under any financial or other obligation to outside individuals or organisations that might influence them in the

performance of their official duties – (Integrity).

They should make choices on merit and on facts – (Objectivity).

They are accountable for their decisions and actions to the public and must submit themselves to whatever scrutiny is appropriate to their office – (Accountability)

They should be as open as possible about all the decisions and actions they take. They should give reasons for their decisions and restrict information only when the wider public interest clearly demands– (Openness).

They have a duty to declare any private interest relating to their public duties and to take steps to resolve any conflicts arising in a way that protects the public interest – (Honesty).

They should promote and support these principles by leadership and example – (Leadership).

Educational institutions can play an important role in the application of these principles in specific cases. They can invite the elected representatives for discussions and dialogue on these points and the elected representatives can help to clarify the application of these principles.

Yet another important fundamental duty is that of protection and improvement of natural environment. Man is part of nature yet in his greed and pride he is causing much destruction to nature. People's representatives will often be faced with the dilemma whether they should support a project which causes environmental damage. On the one hand, there is need for power (electricity), water, employment, etc. and it seems in public interest to support a project that provides these, but on the other, are ecological consequences and long term disasters. The Bhagawad Gita has a beautiful story on this. At the beginning of creation, Prajhapathi, the creator, created men (the prajas) and along with them yajna or sacrifice and told the prajas that through

Yagna you will nourish nature and nature will nourish you and by this mutual nourishment you will prosper and attain all your wishes. By yajna one can mean a ritual, the pouring of ghee over fire dedicated to particular God. Yajna can also be interpreted as sacrifice, the giving of something without any expectation of a return. Viewed in this latter manner, the story of the Gita enjoins man to sacrifice some of the material comforts that he can attain by manipulating nature. In this way, he can nourish nature and if he does so, nature will nourish him. If on the other hand, he continues to exploit nature to "raise" his standard of living endlessly he becomes a cancer cell on nature's body and he will destroy nature, and himself in the process.

Hence it is the duty of the elected representative to fight for protection of nature which means fight against consumerism and ever increasing use of electric power and oil energy for raising the standards of living. It means raising questions about the meaning of "consumption" and standard of living, and educating the public to apply moderation in these matters. The mentality of seeking wealth at the cost of everything else has been severely condemned in the Gita as the Asuric mentality that will lead nowhere but to hell. A person with such mentality is described in the Gita as one who boasts "I have attained this much, I will attain very much more, I will accumulate capital, I have killed this enemy, I will kill ever many more, I am the Lord, I am the enjoyee, I will fulfill these works, I am successful, who is equal to me?"

This kind of individual and collective egocentric approaches glorified by the West as "great entrepreneurship" have resulted on the one hand in enormous increase in wealth and scientific innovations and on the other great increase in anxiety, stresses, loneliness, loss of human values and environmental degradation. The roots of ecological destruction are not in science as such, but the perverted definition of human wants perpetrated by media. It is within the power of the elected representatives of the people to educate the people to the contrary and protect and promote our cultural roots which are environment friendly and foster a balanced approach to life.

Yet another duty as specified in Article 51A (I) is to safeguard public property and to abjure violence. Loss of life and property in riots and agitations have reached enormous proportions. The very process of democracy requires that we attend to matters by dialogue and consensus and not through controversies and violence. The elected representatives have to educate their followers and supporters on the importance of the processes of reasoning and dialogue and avoid steps that lead to violence of any kind.

The role of the elected representative in relation to Fundamental Duties may at first sight seem contributory and complex. He is supposed to represent and promote the common interest of the people yet he has to educate, restrain and moderate them. He has to work for the poor and for greater equality, yet he has to promote the creation of wealth. He has to ensure education for all, yet he has to work for excellence. He must be firmly rooted in his own way of life and culture, yet show regard for all cultures and ways of life. He has to look to the interests of his constituents, yet he must act in larger interest of the country and his conscience. These opposite polarities do not create a conflict. Only a wealthy society can create equality, only a society that pursues merit and excellence can create an educated society. Only a society which pursues Dharma and yajna (sacrifice) can create a truly wealthy society. Through moderation, balance, education and leadership, the elected representatives of the people can lead the country on the path to genuine progress that balances these polarities. For fulfilling these roles envisaged for elected representatives, elected representatives should work closely with the educational institutions in their constituencies and create a network of activities and programmes that generate an understanding of the Fundamental Duties and their application in our day to day life.

In parliament, orientation programmes for new members are organised and senior and outstanding parliamentarians speak to the new members regarding the role of various institutions, raising of matters of public importance and how to function effectively in the Parliament to achieve public good. The Members are also made aware of their role and privileges. The State governments are having similar programmes in some of their Legislatures. There are also many institutions based programmes and seminars for orientation of Parliament Members /legislatures. In all these programmes there should be an adequate emphasis on the role of Members of Parliament and Legislators in promoting the understanding and observance of Fundamental Duties and how to utilize schools and other educational institutions for this purpose.

For the functioning of the pacnayat and municipal programmes, State governments have devised some training courses. The National Institute of Rural Development, Rajendra Nagar, Hyderabad, organizes programmes for community participation, school sanitation, drinking water quality, water related diseases, motivation, sanitation, technologies and techniques and so on. Most of the States have similar institutions under the aegis of Department of Rural Development. Some of the institutions are as old as the Community Development Programme in the times of the then Union Minister, S.K. Dey in the fifties. These institutions, over the years, lost much of the shine of the Community Development and Training. The 73rd and 74th Amendments while revamping the Panchyati Raj could be seen as an opportunity to upgrade and modernize training systems of elected representatives of the district and other levels. This had become necessary since additional responsibilities were being conferred upon panchayat and municipal bodies by the State governments. It was necessary that the functionaries were aware of their role vis-à-vis requirements and demands of modern times. Unless the vision was conveyed and methods for realisation explained, it might not be possible to get the programmes translated into action at those levels. The training could give an understanding for interaction with administration as well as the masses, and speed up the programmes of immediate local need. The village and municipal bodies could design and execute schemes at their levels without the need to always look to the State or the Central capital.

All these orientation programmes at various levels for the elected representatives should emphasise in adequate measure an understanding of Fundamental Duties and the role of the elected representatives in ensuring or promoting the observance of Fundamental Duties by all citizens. In doing so, it should be emphasised that the elected representatives can make a significant contribution by interaction with the younger generation especially through the schools.

# 5

# Public Administration: Civil Services

*S.B. Lal*

Though for teaching of Fundamental Duties to the citizens of the country programme packages for educational institutions from the primary to the university levels should be developed and implemented, such programmes could also be developed through training and professional institutions meant for different professions. As civil services have a vital role to play in our democratic polity, they could become a very important means of teaching and implementing the Fundamental Duties enshrined in the Constitution to other citizens apart from themselves carrying out those duties as good citizens.

## Role of Civil Services

With the achievement of Independence and the adoption of the Constitution, the whole structure of the government in India changed from an autocratic structure to a democratic one. The administrative system had now to function in the context of democracy, development and decentralisation. This cast a heavy responsibility on the shoulders of the public servants whose role had to be radically reoriented. The new multi-disciplinary bureaucracy required men of vision, ability and competence, efficiency, honesty and integrity, neutrality and impartiality as well as anonymity committed to the service of the people and suitable for bringing about the required socio-economic change. On the whole, the Constitution made provisions which were intended to build up a system of public services which would fit into the changed character of the State in India. The loyalty or commitment of this bureaucracy is not to any individual or government in power but to the Constitution. As citizens of the country themselves, the civil servants have to be committed to the service of the citizens at large.

Fully realising the importance of civil services in the modern democratic State, the founding fathers made necessary provisions in the Constitution outlining the role, rights and obligations for those citizens who join the public services. The Constitution provides for selection to public services on merit, for their security of service and tenure and protection against arbitrary dismissal, removal or reduction in rank and for safeguards and opportunity to defend themselves. In this connection, the Constitution also provides for the setting up of an independent Public Service Commission for the Union and for each of the States, and the creation of All India Services, keeping in view the importance of fostering the concepts of national integration, one citizenship and the Union as a single administrative unit. The Constitution gave the power to the Legislature to regulate the recruitment and conditions of service of public servants. The exercise of this power is subject to the various other provisions of the Constitution which ensure that the Fundamental Rights of the citizens offering themselves for public service are not compromised.

## Size and Crucial Importance of Civil Services

With the adoption of the concepts of Welfare State and socialist pattern, the sphere of government has expanded enormously since 1947 resulting in an immense increase in the strength of the civil services. The number of central government civil servants rose from 14.45 lakh on April 1, 1948 to 33.7 lakh in 1996. It is estimated that the number of civil servants employed in the States was 74.1 lakh; more than double of the number of employees in the central government. In addition, 64.6 lakh persons were employed in the Central-State public sector and other quasi-government undertakings.

**Employment in Public Sector**

*(in lakh)*

| *End of March* | *Central Govt.* | *State Govt.* | *Quasi Govt.* | *Total** |
|---|---|---|---|---|
| 1961 | 20.9 | 30.1 | 7.7 | 70.5 |
| 1991 | 34.1 | 71.1 | 62.2 | 190.6 |
| 1996 | 33.7 | 74.1 | 64.6 | 194.3 |

* Including Local Bodies

(Statistical Outline of India 1998-99. Tata Services Ltd.)

Thus, about two crore citizens were working as civil servants in the country in 1996. The impact that this important class of citizens had over other citizens was much more than their size dictated as they were spread over all levels of administration i.e. from the village level, the taluk level, the district level, the State level to the level of the central government. They exercised powers and authority derived from various laws, rules and regulations. Their importance arose from the following functions that they and only they could perform:

(i) As a constitutional institution for ensuring law and order in society, they were wedded to the task of defending the unity and integrity of the country against recalcitrant neighbour and misguided internal saboteurs. They promoted peace, stability and tranquility, without which no economic, social, political or creative activity could ever flourish.

(ii) They enforced socially beneficial regulations with reference to crucial inputs like land, forests, minerals, energy, water, finance, manpower, training, education, health, housing and the like. They could hasten the setting up of infrastructure, speed up economic growth and provide a boost to national and international trade.

(iii) They were catalytic agents for change. They were an educated and well qualified group of people with a presence right up to the grass-roots. They had access to information from all over the world; they had the means to implement ideas and they had the communication network to propagate their agenda for action.

(iv) They provided inputs for the maintenance of the macro-economic equilibrium such as encouraging modern management and technology in agriculture, industry and services.

(v) As watchdogs, they were capable of regulating the actions of all the players and ensuring a level playing field. They could support the good people and suppress the malefactors.

The civil services thus played crucial role in the national life.

## Training of Civil Servants and Fundamental Duties

Over the years, elaborate and sophisticated systems of pre-entry, orientation, postentry and in-service training have been adopted in academies of administration and training institutions for services under the Central and the State governments. A suitable module relating to the Fundamental Duties enshrined in the Constitution must be made a part of the courses in all the civil services training institutions. This module should lay emphasis on the constitutional character and importance of the Fundamental Duties of citizens as also on the relationship between

Fundamental Rights and Directive Principles of State Policy. It may be noted that Fundamental Rights are in the nature of legally enforceable guarantees and the Directive Principles are in the nature of guidelines and assurances, both of them by the State to the citizens.

On the other hand, Fundamental Duties embodied in Article 51A are moral assurances of citizens to citizens; they are not enforceable in courts of law. The civil servants should be sensitised to the basic need for carrying out the Fundamental Duties during their entire careers. This is as important as teaching them the aims and obligations of the civil services and the ethics of the profession: objectivity, honesty, integrity, thoughtfulness, impartiality and neutrality. Thus, the civil servants who constitute a very important part of our total population can be made to imbibe the Fundamental Duties and implement the same in actual practice as citizens. As each member of the civil service comes into contact with a number of other citizens during the course of his duty he can make them realise the importance of following the Fundamental Duties by his own personal conduct.

## Suggested Module for Training of Civil Servants

Over the years detailed training programmes have been prepared in the training institutions for the civil servants keeping in view their job requirements and the levels at which they operate. The civil servants in the central government are distributed in different groups as follows:

| | |
|---|---|
| Group A | 1.9% |
| Group B | 3.2% |
| Group C | 67.1% |
| Group D | 27.2% |
| Unclassified | 0.5% |

Thus, most of the civil servants who are being trained are in Groups C & D. For senior officers belonging to Group

A & B, refresher and orientation courses are also organised and study leave is granted to enable them to increase their skills and to broaden their vision. The module for training civil servants in Fundamental Duties has to be devised keeping in view their levels of operations. This module should cover workshops and discussions on the following subjects:

1. Culture of the Indian Constitution – values enshrined in the Preamble and other Articles of the Constitution.
2. Citizen's Fundamental Rights.
3. Directive Principles of State Policy.
4. Fundamental Duties:
   (a) Relationship to Fundamental Rights
   (b) Fundamental Duties of the citizens listed in Article 51A can be categorised as follows:
      (i) Duties relating to political integrity (clauses a, c & d)
         (a) to abide the Constitution and respect its ideals and institutions, the National Flag and the National Anthem;
         (c) to uphold and protect the sovereignty, unity and integrity of India;
         (d) to defend the country and render national service when called upon to do so.
      (ii) Duties to preserve and perpetuate our cultural heritage (clauses b, e & f)
         (b) to cherish and follow the noble ideals which inspired our national struggle for freedom;
         (e) to promote harmony and the spirit of common brotherhood amongst all the people of India transcending religious, linguistic and regional or sectional diversities; to renounce practices derogatory to the dignity of women;

(f) value and preserve the rich heritage of our composite culture.

(iii) Duties to develop and maintain high quality of life (clauses g, h, i and j)

(g) to protect and improve the natural environment including forests, lakes, rivers, wild life and to have compassion for living creatures;

(h) to develop the scientific temper, humanism and the spirit of inquiry and reform;

(i) to safeguard public property and to abjure violence;

(j) to strive towards excellence in all spheres of individual and collective activity so that the nation constantly rises to higher levels of endeavour and achievement;

(k) Parent or guardian to provide opportunities for education to his child or, as the case may be, ward between the age of six and fourteen years.

While discussing the above duties, it may be emphasised that each duty calls for some action on the part of the trainee. It requires moulding of our behaviour in a particular way. For instance, show of respect for the National Anthem would mean observance of the following norms:

- When the National Anthem is sung or played, everyone should stand at attention. To move or talk while the National Anthem is sung, is highly disrespectful;
- One should know the words and meaning of the National Anthem and be able to sing it correctly;
- While singing in chorus, sing in unision and with full vigour;
- Show respect to the National Anthem everywhere,

and on all occasions, by standing erect, motionless and by singing in tune.

Real citizenship education lies not only in knowing but also in doing and becoming; therefore, after they have done the above mentioned exercise, let the trainees simulate individual and group activity in which they practise the observance of the laid down norms.

To learn the difference between a legal duty and a moral duty, let them now list out all the legal duties and moral duties that they can think of. Each one of them will do this exercise. Make the final list out of the lists prepared by individuals, through discussion.

Each one of the trainees will then check which legal duties and which moral duties they as individual citizens have not carried out.

Honesty and sincerity are the core of this activity and, therefore, the discussion that should be carried on during the activity should be frank and open.

## Achieving Excellence by Public Servants as Citizens

In Clause (j) of Article 51A of the Constitution which lays down that it shall be duty of every citizen of India "to strive towards excellence in all spheres of individual and collective activity so that the nation constantly rises to higher levels of endeavour and achievement", is of special significance as the conduct of civil servants is of crucial importance for the society and the country. To what extent have the civil servants as citizens succeeded in striving towards excellence in their sphere of activity?

After over 60 years of working of the Constitution, we can now evaluate to what extent the aims and objectives of the founding fathers in regard to the civil services have been achieved. It has, however, to be appreciated that the responsibility for the country's achievements and failures has to be borne both by the Nation's political leaders as well as civil servants. We can be justifiably proud and happy on our achievements. During the last sixty years we have had fifteen General Elections and over 300 State Elections with increasing voter participation which was over 60 per cent. This compares very favourably with the best of the Western democracies. Unlike many of the other developing countries, transfer of power to successive governments in India has been smooth and peaceful. We have succeeded not only in winning and enlarging our political freedom and ensuring record performance of the country as a successfully functioning democracy, we have also been able to safeguard the country's territorial integrity and sovereignty, consolidate our unity in diversity and lay solid foundations for economic prosperity and social progress.

While we have, in part, realised the vision of the founding fathers of our Constitution, we have, at the same time, to lament with anguish the tremendous shortfalls in reaching the targets set by them in the areas of democratic governance, economic performance, human development and international influence. Consequently, we are faced with gigantic problems such as over-population, stark poverty and wide-spread illiteracy which are complicated by "casteism, communalism, corruption and criminalisation – all increasingly politicised".

The changing scenario in the past 60 years of public administration has placed several challenges before the public services. One of the major ones is the steady downward trend in ethical standards all around the country. While the services cannot bear the entire responsibility for the general environment, they have necessarily to face the problems thrown up by the stifling atmosphere. They cannot shy away from their duty of devising ways and means to meet this challenge in public administration.

Corruption in public life and administration is on the increase and quite rapidly too. This has resulted in widespread dissatisfaction among the people especially the poor and the weaker sections. The public servant is today viewed as a monument of apathy and unresponsiveness. There appears to be a total lack of accountability on the part of public servants. Every right thinking citizen, especially the people at the helm of affairs, are expected to show a greater concern for ensuring clean, responsive, transparent and people friendly administration at all levels. It is high time, everyone concerned with the issue of ethics and values in public life must initiate the necessary corrective steps to ensure that the administration is viewed as free from corruption and responsive to the expectations and problems of the society especially those of the vulnerable groups.

## Concrete Suggestions for Operationalisation of Fundamental Duties by Civil Servants

Mentioned below are specific areas in which suitable intervention could ensure that public servants themselves implement the Fundamental Duties laid down in Article 51A in an exemplary manner so that public service is viewed as credible and to a great extent principled institution, responsible towards the citizens of the country in a democratic set up. Public service has to be accountable to the people. Accountability primarily means an honest and transparent administration adhering to the highest possible standards of moral principles for bringing about an effective and qualitative improvement in the lives of the citizens. Accordingly, it is essential that the following issues be addressed and steps as suggested below initiated:

(i) An attempt should be made to inculcate a missionary spirit in all public servants. Public service should be regarded as a mission for improving the lives of citizens while upholding the highest moral and ethical values. Every new entrant in public service should be administered with a pledge for specifically implementing Fundamental Duties laid down in Article 51A of the Constitution;

(ii) All civil servants should be given training in the implementation of Fundamental Duties. The courses followed in the training institutions for civil services for induction training should include a module for such training. This should be devised keeping in view their level of operation in society and on the lines suggested in paragraph 6 above;

(iii) All Heads of Departments/offices and supervisory officers should review the implementation of Fundamental Duties in their organisations at the regular monthly/quarterly review meetings and give suitable guidance and directions to the staff;

(iv) It should be made obligatory on the part of all reporting and reviewing officers to make, while recording the Annual Confidential Report of every civil servant, a specific appreciation of the implementation of Fundamental Duties by him;

(v) Emphasis should be placed on the importance of presenting the human face of the administration. This is possible if Fundamental Duties are strictly followed. It should be the responsibility of the senior public servants to project the image of administration as people friendly and responsive to the problems and sufferings of the citizens;

(vi) All public servants should attach a high degree of importance to developing good and positive human relations. They should be easily approachable;

(vii) The Government should move towards giving greater access to information to members of the public. One of the major reasons for inefficiency and corruption in government is the secrecy that shrouds most of the decision making processes. Transparency and free supply of information will reduce corruption and ensure accountability;

(viii) In order to implement Fundamental Duty (j) of Article 51A in the sphere of public administration, it is essential to make a sincere attempt to root out corruption at different levels. Secretaries to Government, Managing Directors in the Public Sector, Heads of Offices/Field Units should be made squarely and personally responsible for taking detailed measures for rooting out corruption in their assigned areas of responsibility. A set of guidelines could be supplied to them for strict compliance. A computerised check should be kept on proven complaints of corruption pertaining to their areas, as recorded in a Central Complaint Cell, and this should be appropriately recorded in their personal files and should be a determining factor for promotions, compulsory retirements, extensions and future employment. They should be shifted out, if they are found waiting in their present job in eliminating corruption in areas under their control;

(ix) Administration at all levels should provide an effective and quick grievance redressal system. Apart from fixing responsibility at every level for dealing with grievances there should be in built mechanism for handling cases of dereliction of duty by public servants where a public grievance has not been redressed within a stipulated time. This will lead to an attitudinal change among those in the public service. The above suggestions could be incorporated in the operational programme for teaching Fundamental Duties to the civil servants as citizens and through them to the other citizens.

# 6

# Administration of Justice

*K.V. Vishwanathan*

The chapter on Fundamental Duties in the Constitution of India could appropriately be called the "Ten (now eleven) commandments". Couched in the plainest of words that English language can offer, they are pregnant with meaning and content, making them inviolable and non-negotiable. "Society" above "Self" may be its exhortation to the citizens, but it consciously creates a no loss and all win situation for him, as in the longer run, by putting "Society" first, it is the "Self" that stands enhanced and reaps the tangible benefits. For the administration of justice, these are touchstones for ready application and if any or all of these commands are used as yard-sticks by the components who participate in the process of administration of justice, to test the correctness of their actions, they could be rest assured that they have discharged their duty ably and without blemish. But who are these components? At first blush, when we talk of administration of justice, it would appear that only the Magistrates, Judges and Lawyers are participants in the process. A closer examination reveals that though judges and lawyers are the visible participants, who apply law to a given fact situation, the entire citizenry is involved in this sphere of activity. It is the common man who resorts to the legal process to assert his "right" and correspondingly to enforce a co-relative "duty" vested in the other. Then you have the lawmakers, who lay down laws that regulate human conduct, and civil servants and law enforcement agencies who administer and enforce laws. In a sense, the effectiveness of the process of administration of justice would be a qualitative basis to gauge the value attached to Fundamental Duties by the citizenry. In other words, the manner of administration of justice would be a true reflection, a mirror image as it were, of the quality of the society. The target group, may be wide and varied but that only makes the task of disseminating information about the invaluableness of the Fundamental Duties, more challenging as very soon the results will be there for one and all to see and relish.

When we talk of administration of Justice, it is advisable to maintain a distinction between the efficacy of the system and the result brought about by its abuse. Not a little finger has been raised against the need for laws to regulate human behaviour, the need for law enforcement agencies to protect the person and property of the citizen, the need for lawyers to espouse the cause of their clients and above all the need for an independent judiciary to adjudicate cases. We have all of it in our country. We are a democracy governed by the rule of law and the Constitution guarantees an independent judiciary; we have the Supreme Court at New Delhi and the High Courts in all the States; a district court for every district and courts of magistrates and civil judges in virtually every nook and corner of the country. There is in every state capital, a legislative assembly to make laws for the state and at the centre we have the Parliament, which makes laws for the entire nation. The Central Government and the State Governments administer the laws and have their enforcement agencies. There are lawyers practising all over the country to help and guide the citizens. The system is timetested and sound and people have utmost faith in it as not only that the existence of the system has not been questioned, there is a demand for establishing more courts and setting up of more police stations. Our country has produced nation-builders of the greatest quality in every walk of life – able parliamentarians, police officers and civil servants of high ability and integrity and judges and lawyers of great intellect.

Having said that, we should not be blind to the realities that exist today. On account of the abuse of the system of administration of justice, for which each one of us is to be blamed, cynicism has set in the society. Citizens today are mortally scared to litigate for their own rights. The common refrain is that, one would not like to be "entangled" in litigation and get 'sucked' into the "vortex' of the court process, for a good part of life would be lost in it. For many, resort to the administration of Justice is a 'far cry' and a 'luxury' they can ill afford. They say law is the convenience of the rich and the lawyer, a person engaged to prove that black is white and white is black, accordingly as he is paid. The criminal-politician nexus and corruption among those administering and enforcing the law are freely discussed. Even the judiciary is not spared, though criticism is in hushed tones. All of it is not false and sadly most of it is true. We need not throw our hands up in despair, as we are a great nation with vast human resources. The degeneration ought to be and can be arrested. 'Where there is a will, there is a way' is an old and oft-quoted adage. It is here that the 'Fundamental Duties', could be deployed to perk-up our drooping spirits.

Creating awareness about the importance of Fundamental Duties to the constituents of the process of administration of justice would in itself ensure the quality of the end product. This is because every Indian is basically "humane" and has the "innate" quality to put "public rights" or in other words, the rights of the society above his personal desires. How else do you explain the co-existence of the citizens of this great country in spite of religious, linguistic, cultural and hundreds of other diversities? "Tolerance" is a virtue, which comes naturally to us. Mild sanctions may have to be prescribed to tackle small aberrations, but they will be only incidental. The message that the Constitution expects compliance to its "commandments" before any claim to exercise the fundamental rights or any other rights is raised has to be conveyed to every citizen. Dissemination of information about Fundamental Duties will go a long way in keeping the wheels of the administration of Justice well-oiled so that the journey is smooth and not turbulent.

Indoctrinating the importance of the Constitutional Values of sovereignty, socialism, secularism, democracy governed by a rule of law, social, economic and political justice, liberty, equality and fraternity and inculcating respect for the dignity of the individual and constitutional institutions is bound to transform any individual – be he a lawyer, a judge, a police officer or a litigant by broadening his vision and thereby changing his approach and outlook to the task on hand. Selflessness and Sacrifice–the two main ideals which inspired our national struggle for freedom – should be the spirit in which public duty is to be discharged. The legal community including the law enforcement agencies should come down very heavily upon any acts of violence, particularly those resulting in damage to public property, flora and fauna. Threats to sovereignty and country should be put down with an iron hand and a collective effort should be made so that the nation constantly rises higher levels of endeavour and achievement. One of the "Commandments" is to develop a scientific temper, which in today's context would mean keeping peace with the development of technology. Use of computers and Internet as well as the need of resorting to speedier modes of communication like e-mail, should be introduced to quicken and render more efficient the process of administration of justice. The administrative wing of the court Management should be headed by officers trained in court techniques.

The Supreme Court has already set the trend is adopting the Fundamental Duties as yardsticks for testing the correctness of laws and actions of those administering the laws. This approach should trickle down to every judicial officer in the country. A judge conscious of Fundamental Duties will surely approach the problem at hand from a broad national perspective rather than the narrow aspect of adjudicating individual rights. Consciousness of Fundamental Duties will help him in unfolding new dimensions to legal provisions. He will start looking beyond the letters of the law and search for the spirit, so will a lawyer. He will realize that judicial time wasted is really public money wasted and he will not unnecessarily prolong the conduct of the case. Consciousness about the importance of the institution, of which he is a part, will dissuade him from advising his client to pursue frivolous litigation. A litigant informed of Fundamental Duties will soon find that the society no longer fears the court process. Government is the largest litigant in the country and individuals in the government take decisions. Holding Fundamental Duties dear to their heart, would change their attitude too.

Who does not want:

- A strong and independent Judiciary where justice is quick and easily accessible to the economically under-privileged living in the remotest corners of this big country,
- Lawyers who carry on their 'profession' and not 'business' and who value the interest of their client more than their own,
- Civil servants who shun the 'red-tape',
- A police force which is honest, fearless and independent, and
- Parliamentarians who are 'Statesmen' and not mere 'politicians'.

How do we go about the task of spreading the message about the importance of the "Fundamental Duties", to the constituency with which we are concerned? The first exercise would be to identify the target groups and thereafter suggest methods. Keeping in mind the goal of an efficient administration of justice the target groups could be:

(a) Law college teachers and students,

(b) Lawyers including government law officers,

(c) Judges, and

(d) Court Officers – the administrative wing of the courts,

(e) Law makers, Law enforcement agencies and litigants.

**Law College Teachers and Students**

Law Colleges are institutions from which Lawyers and Judges are produced. Teaching Fundamental Duties in an organized manner in law Colleges would go a long way in toning up the administration of justice. Some suggestions are given herein below:

- While recruiting students for the law colleges, special emphasis on Fundamental Duties must be laid in the entrance examination and in the viva-voce. Questions on constitutional values and Fundamental Duties at least to the extent of 50 marks must be prescribed in the entrance examination;
- The aspects of Fundamental Duties must be appropriately classified so that both in the 3 year course and 5 year course, this subject is taught every year and the students are examined on the subject to a maximum of 100 marks;
- Writing of monographs and articles on various aspects of constitutional values with special emphasis on Fundamental Duties must be made compulsory and should be one of the criterion for promotion to the next year;
- Moot court on issues involving application of Fundamental Duties for resolution, must be organized every year and participation in it should be made compulsory;
- Leading members of the bar, jurists, serving and

retired members of the higher and the subordinate judiciary must be invited by every law college to address the students on various aspects of law with special emphasis on Fundamental Duties. A scheme should be formulated by the university to which the college is affiliated, whereunder the visiting members are treated as visiting faculty. This will ensure that not only the students learn in depth the various intent of Fundamental Duties, but the visiting faculty also gets an opportunity to delve deep into the various aspects;

- As far as the permanent faculty members are concerned, both at the time of their initial recruitment and at the time of their in-service promotion, special emphasis on Fundamental Duties should be given and only those with a track record of contribution towards dissemination of information on Fundamental Duties, like participation in seminars and writing of articles on the subject, should be recruited and promoted;
- Members of the permanent faculty should be associated in the process of continuing education, which has been prescribed herein below for lawyers, judges and members of the law enforcement agencies;
- The members of the permanent faculty should organize seminars on constitutional values with special emphasis on Fundamental Duties and the hosting of seminars must be made compulsory and should form a criteria for their further promotion;
- Students of the final year and the members of the permanent faculty must co-opt with the local bar association and the social service organizations like Rotary Club, the Lions Club, etc. to organize legal clinics to apprise the general citizenry and the litigant public of the need for adherence to Fundamental Duties. In this process the executive machinery

functioning in the area headed by the District Magistrate / Collector and the police force headed by Superir 'endent of Police should be involved. Participation in a minimum number of legal clinics must be made compulsory for enabling a student to sit for the final examination and correspondingly for the District Magistrate and Superintendent of Police for their career advancement;

- In the interim report of the Justice Verma Committee, a salutary suggestion ismade that biographies of the builders of modern India should be included in the curricula for schools and colleges. Books on stalwarts in the field of law and other leading texts on professional conduct and advocacy must be prescribed in the syllabi of law colleges. The following books must be made a compulsory study:
  - (a) Professional Conduct and Advocacy – by Sri K.V. Krishnaswamy Aiyar;
  - (b) A Statesman among Jurists – Biography of Sri Alladi Krishnaswamy by Sri Alladi Kuppuswamay;
  - (c) To the Best of My Memory – Autobiography of Chief Justice Gajendragadkar;
  - (d) My Own Boswell – Autobiography of Chief Justice Hidayatullah;
  - (e) My Life, Law and Other Things – Autobiography of Sri Motilal Setalved – First Attorney General for India;
  - (f) Roses in December – Autobiography of Chief Justice M.C. Chagla.
- From the first year, to develop respect for the constitutional institutions, law college students must be taken on visits to the local courts, High Courts and the Supreme Court. For poor and indigent

students, State funding must be provided;

- Legal philanthropists and leading members of the bar must be persuaded to set up chairs in universities for pursuing research on various aspects of Fundamental Duties. Tax incentives for any endowment set up by them should be generously given;
- Every college must have a monthly bulletin setting out the activities of the college and the bulletin must carry articles on various aspects of Fundamental Duties;
- In any activity undertaken by the college in this regard, the print and electronic media must be associated, so that wide publicity is given;
- In all the legal textbooks published by the Government, in the college bulletin and the college dairy, the clauses of Fundamental Duties should be prominently set out. The preamble to the Constitution and the ten clauses of article 51A relating to the Fundamental Duties should be prominently displayed in the law colleges and in the universities. January 3 of every year should be observed in the colleges as Fundamental Duties Day and the students and teachers must solemnly read out and affirm the clauses of article 51A relating to Fundamental Duties;
- Post-graduate studies on Fundamental Duties and Award of Doctorate for research work on Fundamental Duties must be encouraged.

**Lawyers including Government Law Officers**

- The practice of subscribing to an oath during enrolment, which is prevalent in some state bar councils should be made universal in application. The oath should lay special emphasis on constitutional values including the Fundamental Duties. On the day of enrolment, lectures should be organized on

Fundamental Duties and participation therein must be made compulsory;

- Membership in bar association should be by way of an interview by the office-bearers, wherein the candidate must be questioned on the various aspects of Fundamental Duties;
- A scheme must be devised whereby the bar associations are affiliated to the Bar Council in the State Headquarters and the Bar Council must provide grants to deserving bar associations for the purpose of conducting monthly seminars on the various aspects of Fundamental Duties and also to enable the bar associations all over the country to invite men and women learned in the field of law to give talks on the contents of Fundamental Duties. The scheme should insist on the local bar association hosting minimum number of seminars and talks, the failure of which will result in de-affiliation and withdrawal of grants. The money for the grants should come from the State government which may reimburse itself of the whole or substantial part of it by increasing the stamp duty on every Vakalatnama and Affidavit filed in court, by a sum not exceeding Rs.1;
- The bar association must compulsorily, for retaining its affiliation, publish a monthly bulletin / magazine;
- Every member to retain his membership in the bar association, must contribute at least one article every year on Fundamental Duties and submit it to the editorial committee of the local bar association;
- The bar association must function in close co-ordination with the faculty of the nearest law college as well as in close coordination with the law enforcement agencies and social service organizations like Rotary and Lions Clubs. The bar association in coordination must organize legal clinics in villages

and towns within its jurisdiction, for the purpose of enlightening the citizens and the litigant public about the importance of Fundamental Duties. Participation by the members in a minimum number of such legal clinics should be made compulsory for continuation of membership and for becoming office bearers in the association;

- The bar council must supervise the functioning of the bar association in this regard and prepare yearly reports and publish the same in its magazine. Recognition should be given to the bar association which has been the most active in the sphere. Criteria for eligibility to be an office bearer in the Bar Council must be framed in such a way that those who have been Office Bearers in their Bar association in the preceding year are rendered eligible;
- For appointment as public prosecutors, government panel lawyers and panel lawyers for banks and public sector corporations, and for appointment as any other law officer of the government as well as for designation as Senior Advocates, participation in legal clinics, seminars and publication of at least two articles on various aspects of Fundamental Duties in recognized journals should be made a condition precedent;
- The bar council of the State should frame a scheme for compulsory continuous education for lawyers on various aspects of law with special emphasis on Fundamental Duties. There must be a system of examination of the lawyers at the end of every course;
- The bar council of every State must publish a monthly magazine, exclusively devoting one part to articles on Fundamental Duties;
- Every bar association must prominently display the preamble and clauses of the Article 51A in the

premises of the bar association;

- On 3rd January every year, the bar association must organize a function after court hours, to commemorate the Fundamental Duties day. Members of the judiciary must be invited and the members of the bench and bar must solemnly read out the clauses of the Fundamental Duties;
- Dairies, calendars, etc. published by the bar association must set out the clauses of Fundamental Duties;
- The editorial committee of every bar association must ensure that the gist of every judgment applying the principles of Fundamental Duties is published in the bulletin of the bar association.

**Judges**

- Criteria for appointment and promotion in the subordinate judiciary must be framed by the High Court in such a manner that the incumbent is made to focus on constitutional values with special emphasis on the intent of Fundamental Duties;
- Judges must be trained under any scheme for continuing education which the High Court may evolve on the following aspects:
  - (a) To apply the principles enshrined in the Fundamental Duties as tools of interpretation while interpreting laws for adjudication of disputes;
  - (b) To recognize and compensate public interest litigants who litigate for enforcing the Fundamental Duties;
  - (c) To impose heavy costs on those persons who show utter disregard to Fundamental Duties;
  - (d) To award maximum punishment for persons causing damage to public property, sexual

offenders, persons violating environment laws, persons committing anti-national acts and persons showing disrespect to national flag and national anthem;

(e) To draft by turn the services of active practitioners as Amicus Curiae for assisting the court in matters involving enforcement of Fundamental Duties and recognizing their services.

- Compilation of the judgments of the Supreme Court and the High Court on aspects of Fundamental Duties should be made available to every judicial officer periodically;
- In the recently set up judicial academy special emphasis should be laid on teaching the technique of applying Fundamental Duties for adjudication of disputes;
- Just as the legislative and executive wings must show respect to the judiciary, the judiciary must also be appraised of the compulsions and constraints of the other two organs so that mutual respect is generated for the constitutional institutions;
- Since Article 51A(h) speaks of developing 'scientific temper' which in today's context would mean keeping in tune with the scientific advancement, judges must be trained in the use of computers and in accessing the Internet so that judicial time is not wasted.

**Court Officers - Administrative Wing of the Court**

The administrative wing of the court is a very essential component of the administration of justice. They must also be conscious of the importance of Fundamental Duties. They can achieve excellence by adopting court management techniques and by training themselves in computers and by familiarizing with the latest modes of communication. There must be a scheme whereby atleast one officer is sponsored for study in management to the Indian Institute of Management. Court management must be made a separate subject, which would deal with classification of cases and other management techniques so that they aid the speedy disposal of cases on the judicial side. The officers must be apprised of the values of Fundamental Duties during such management classes and on their return they must be made to address other court staff and by this process the chain of learning must be kept going.

**Law Makers and Law Enforcement Agencies and Litigants**

The interim report of the Justice Verma Committee in chapter IV had called for enactment of suitable legislation to require obedience to the obligations by the citizens, backed by legal sanctions, while at the same time ensuring faithful and effective implementation of the existing legislation. Legislators and Parliamentarians have the right to introduce private member's bills. They must be inspired to use their originality and creativity in coming out with legislation to further the objects of Fundamental Duties by identifying the mischief and suggesting remedial measures. Similarly, the law enforcement agencies and civil servants must be continuously apprised of the importance of the Fundamental Duties. Respect for the institution of Judiciary should be emphasized and the need for proper and speedy implementation of court orders must be highlighted. Inmates of jails should be taught the value of adhering to Fundamental Duties and remission of sentences should be recommended based on the cooperation of the participants. A wing under the supervision of the State Chief Secretary and the Union Cabinet Secretary must be set up to educate the civil servants and the police. For the police there exist already academies where they are trained on various matters concerning their profession. Special attention should be focused on Fundamental Duties in academics and in-service promotion should depend on their active participation in spreading the message of Fundamental

Duties. Government should set up an institute for studies on Fundamental Duties and offer research scholarships. As far as the litigant is concerned, the legal clinics suggested above should inculcate in him the need for compliance with Fundamental Duties. The valuable experience of the members of the Law Commission of India should be utilized to recommend proposed legislation to enforce the Fundamental Duties. Similarly the research scholars at the Indian Law Institute and other recognized legal bodies must be requested to publish well-researched papers on various aspects of Fundamental Duties.

Administration of justice being a facet of every civilized society can only be as good as the society is which in turn would depend on how good the citizens are. A solemn and sincere resolve to adopt the Fundamental Duties as "code of conduct" to regulate our day to day behaviour is bound to ensure greater mental and social peace and an advancement in the quality of life, resulting in complete satisfaction even to the innermost recesses of our minds. Is not adherence to Fundamental Duties the most simple and sensible investment one would have ever made?

# 7

# Business and Industry

***Brij Mohan*** **and** ***D.N. Saxena***

## I. Profile of Business Sectors: Strengths and Weaknesses

In a generic sense, the term 'Business' covers a wide spectrum of activities, the central objective there being to generate income, which should in turn lead to further accretion of wealth in the community. While among the individuals and enterprises undertaking these activities, there is bound to be a large measure of variation in matters such as form of organisation, nature and variety of products, scale of operations and ownership profile, a common thread running all through is the quest for maximisation of return on investment on one hand and genuine expectation for securing an adequate regard for entrepreneurial inputs on the other. Profit motive and its necessary concomitant viz. the urge for growth are thus the twin driving forces that keep sustaining and indeed intensifying the dynamism of this sector.

Business accounts for more than fifty percent of India's Net Domestic Product (NDP) and this percentage has been going up from year to year. **This highlights the preponderance of business sector in the economy and also in the society as a whole.**

An important point of strength of business is that it does have at **its command relatively better managerial and technical skills as also entrepreneurial** urge than is usually the case with other segments of the society. This does help it to be efficient as well as dynamic. Given the will and commitment, there is no reason why efficiency aspect of business cannot concurrently be harnessed for achieving two somewhat inter-related goals:

(i) realisation of sustained and growing profits on one hand, and

(ii) pursuance as well as promotion of a value based system which embodies not merely protection of one's rights but also rights of others.

The success of a business unit need not always be measured merely in terms of profitability as such but also in terms of its contribution in the area of social action. Business sector is part of the social system. It cannot ignore the overall environment of the system. It has to be sensitive to prevailing environment and has to make its contribution towards promoting a value-based social order, caused and sustained by preservation of social values that a nation confers upon itself through constitutional rights and duties.

The fact is that both the approach and behaviour of a business unit does influence a very large section of the populace. This is because in the very nature of things a business unit has to come inevitably in contact with a number of operators: buyers and suppliers, intermediaries and facilitators, employees and managers, government agencies and their functionaries and investors and shareholders. All of these conditions are in turn conditioned by business perspective and its operational approach.

Business prospers if and when it has a long term perspective and adopts upright practices. Short term gains achieved by deliberate violation of laws of the land and or by disregarding social values that a responsible citizen is expected to pursue are bound to be detrimental to business itself. While these two viz. violation of laws and disregard of values are not misdemeanors of identical nature, the fact is that if a business unit bids good-bye to social values, it then gets gradually entrapped into a vicious circle. One lapse leads to another and the seriousness of lapses in respect of observance of a value system keeps on mounting. A stage then reaches when breaking of laws of the land tends to assume multiple dimensions. In a way this is what is presently happening on a large scale in India. If one analyses the prevailing state of affairs in respect of such aberrations as corruption, bribery and generation of black money, one would find that the starting point for these aberrations happens to be the unethical practice of 'cutting corners' with a view to maximising gains and thus deliberately ignoring the voice of one's own conscience. What is patently wrong cannot be viewed as right nor can a wrong ever be justified by the logic that the type of wrong action that one is indulging in is already being done by others also and that too with impunity.

It is a fact that quite often some business units and entrepreneurs do succumb to the temptation of restoring to unethical practices and then the aberrations so committed become habit forming. How to deal with the vicious circle of aberrations is indeed a serious challenge to the society.

## II. Current Status in Regard to Discharging of Social Responsibilities by Business

Business cannot regard itself as an island unto itself; it is indeed part and parcel of society and as such it has both rights and duties. The Constitution attaches a great deal of importance to citizenship values. The Preamble states that it is the people of India who have resolved to constitute India into a Sovereign Socialist Secular Democratic Republic. Having resolved to do so, it is the same people viz. citizens of the country who should sincerely abide by the ideals and values put forth not only in the Preamble but also in the parts dealing with Fundamental Rights,

Directive Principles of State Policy and Fundamental Duties. Every right has the counterpart in duty. Business is no exception to this equilibrating mechanism and thus business, which gets immensely affected and in turn influenced by the environment in which it operates, has indeed a duty to ensure that environment continues to be healthy, friendly and co-operative so as to make adequate contribution to citizenship values.

While there is no doubt that the prime duty of a business unit is to carry out its operations efficiently so that it is able to supply quality products to consumers at competitive rates, keep all stakeholders happy through its honest dealings with them, pay taxes to government honestly and able to secure adequate return on investment, it is also its duty as a citizen to perform its citizenship duties laid out in the Constitution. Business has obligations towards the community and also towards other fellow citizens. As a profit making organisation and as part of the social system, it should assist the needy and poor sections of the community and also abide by the constitutional provisions defining the citizenship values, in particular fundamental duties. It should set examples of good behaviour so that others in the community may emulate them.

So far, the involvement of business in discharging social responsibilities has basically been in two fields:

(a) assistance to selected local communities in formulating and implementing community development and social welfare programmes; and

(b) pursuance of ethical and moral standards and for that purpose formulation of model code of conduct.

Large business houses, mega size corporations, public sector undertakings and selected multinational companies do recognize that they should on their own take up some constructive work, which would improve income earning capacity of neighbouring communities and instill in the spirit of self-reliance. It is with this objective in mind that some of them have taken up **community development and social welfare programmes.** Generally the pattern is that the parent company sets up a non-profit-making institution – may be a Trust, a Foundation or a Society – charged with the responsibility of undertaking developmental and welfare activities. The funding for the institution is wholly/largely provided by the parent company itself. In some cases, the institution may get financial help from other sources also, including project specific funding support from foreign agencies to be utilised on specific developmental and social welfare programmes and not to be diverted for any other purpose. Typical activities taken up by the institutions of this type are in areas such as agriculture, rural development, social forestry and environmental control, rural energy needs, slum clearance and housing, education, children welfare, minor irrigation, family planning, training of functionaries involved in Panchayati Raj institutions, help to physically impaired, vocational training and special schemes aimed at removal of gender bias and improving the quality of life of women, members of scheduled castes and scheduled tribes and economically backward persons.

In addition to individual companies, some important chambers of commerce and industry associations – basically national and regional ones – have also set up institutions charged with the responsibility of formulating community development and social welfare programmes. Part of the funding for the institutions is usually provided out of the chamber's own budget and the remaining is raised by persuading individual members of the chamber. In some cases the institution concerned may succeed in getting funding support from other sources also, including foreign agencies. It is tied aid and the proceeds have to be utilised only for specific projects/schemes agreed between the donor agency and the recipient one. Any departure from this is not only unethical but also against the legal provisions governing the inflow of foreign contributions.

An important development that emerged during the decade of nineteen nineties is the concern shown by Indian business for upgrading ethical standards in business dealings and thus to acquire for itself a better image both at home and abroad. There are two reasons for this. Firstly, economic reforms and liberalised polices initiated in India since the beginning of 1990's have resulted in reduction of a number of regulatory and licensing provisions, with the result that a new environment has emerged in which business has now an opportunity to play a more active and constructive role in a variety of areas including the area of social action programmes based on ethical values. Secondly, at the global level also, the desirability of the business sincerely pursuing higher ethical standards is being emphasised. Several governmental and non-governmental agencies of the developed countries have come out with suggestions that for the elimination of corruption and pursuance by business of practices that would elevate ethical standards to a higher level, codes or guidelines for ethical conduct should be prepared and the business should then be persuaded to comply with them.

In India, too, important chambers of commerce and industry associations have taken initiative for formulating norms of ethical conduct for business dealings. Given below is a list of norms culled out from the codes formulated by two chambers of commerce and industry: Federation of Indian Chambers of Commerce and Industry (FICCI) and PHD Chamber of Commerce and Industry (PHDCCI).

- The codes formulated by chambers and other agencies are essentially self-regulatory guidelines and not in the nature of mandatory instructions. It is for each organisation to consult one's own conscience and convenience and then take a decision as to which of the suggested norms set out in a code, should one implement and how should the implementation process be managed.

- Business should **conduct its operations in a manner that earns the goodwill of all concerned** – the employees, customers, shareholders and other individuals and organisations and society as a whole.
- **Quality is an important aspect of products.** It is also essential that quality standards are property maintained and to the extent possible, upgraded. However, **one should never claim what one does not possess and that applies to quality also.** As false claim on any substantial point will damage image as also to business itself. Once image gets tarnished business is bound to suffer.
- **Honesty and uprightness on all crucial points and dealings should be the motto for all the business units.**
- Business should avoid **publishing misleading advertisements.**
- Business should use **knowledge and experience for upgradation of quality of life.** All business must **combine the quality of private excellence for public good.**

It is the responsibility of business:

- to maintain accuracy in weights and measures in respect of goods offered for sale;
- to ensure that warranty of a product or service is based on adequate data or test;
- to ensure that products conform to specified standards or accepted norms in regard to safety of products;
- to provide after sales-service for consumer durables;
- not to manufacture, store or sell adulterated goods and

- not to deal knowingly in spurious or smuggled product.

For public sector enterprises[1], a separate Code of Conduct and Ethics has been drafted. The principles incorporated in the code are basically addressed to Chief Executives, Executives, Managers and other employees of the PSEs. Important principles are summarised below:

- Each and every employee[2] of PSEs should maintain the highest standards of probity and integrity;
- While recommending any action, each and every employee should uphold rule of law and respect for human rights solely in public interest;
- Decision taken by each and every employee to be objective and transparent and should not appear to be partisan promoting improper gains to political party in power or for themselves or for anyone else;
- It is the duty of all employees not to frustrate or undermine policies, decisions or action already taken by 'higher authorities', particularly those decisions, which have been judged as being in public interest;
- Where an employee has reasonable grounds to believe that he/she is being required by the superior authority to act in a manner, which is illegal, he/she should in that case decline to implement the recommendation of the superior authority;
- Religion, region, caste and/or language of an executive to have no influence on the working in his official capacity;
- Each and every employee to refrain from taking decisions in respect of which he/she believes that he/ she will benefit any particular person or party at the cost of public interest;
- Each and every employee to disclose any clash of interest when there is conflict between public and

private interest on one hand or when he/she is likely to benefit from any act of omission or commission on his part on the other;

- Employees should be alert to any actual/potential conflict of interest, financial or otherwise, and should disclose this to superiors;
- Each and every employee to maintain his/her independence, dignity and impartiality by not approaching politicians or outsiders;
- Consistent with accountability to superior authorities, employees should practise accountability to the public in terms of equality of service, in time less, courtesy, people orientation and readiness to encourage participation of partnership with citizen groups;
- Each and every employee should be consistent, equitable and honest in his/her treatment of the public with particular care for the weaker sections of the society;
- Decision of employees in pursuit of discretionary powers should be justifiable on the basis of non-arbitrary and objective criteria;
- Each and every employee should recognize and enforce customer's right for speedy redressal of grievances and should commit oneself to provide services of declared quality and standards to customers;
- Employees to respect the right of public to information on all activities and transactions of the organisation except where they are debarred in public interest from releasing information;
- Each and every employee to avoid wastage and extravagance. In case of disputes or grievances, efforts to be made to resolve them quickly. No unlawful stoppage of work or damage to the assets of the PSE's to be resorted to;

- Employees not to abuse their official position to obtain a benefit for themselves or for anyone else. They must take decisions on merit;
- Each and every employee should treat it a duty to continuously upgrade his/her skills and knowledge, strive for creativity and innovation and nurture the values of team working and harmony;
- Each and every employee to promote and exhibit public and private conduct in keeping with the appropriate behaviour and standards of excellence and integrity
- Each and every employee to support the juniors in the latter's efforts to resist wrong or illegal directives and in abiding by the code of ethics. At the same time, each and every employee should reward good work and punish dereliction of duty and work for fulfilling obligations based on objective and transparent criteria.

The code of ethical conduct drafted for PSEs focuses on principles and in this respect is somewhat of an improvement over those formulated by chambers and industry associations. While the desirability of prescribing norms such as 'honesty', 'transparency', 'maintenance of high standards of probity and integrity' is emphasised in the codes of both viz. chambers and associations on one hand and PSE's on the other, what distinguishes the code of the latter is the specific inclusion therein of such norms also as summarised below:

- to uphold rule of law and respect for Human Rights;
- to maintain dignity and impartiality and not to approach politicians or outsiders;
- to be accountable not merely to superiors but also to public;
- to take particular care for weaker sections of the community;

- to continuously upgrade skills and knowledge;
- to attain standards of excellence and dignity.

The involvement of financial sector viz. commercial banks, insurance companies and other financial institutions in social action programmes follows a pattern from that of business units discussed so far. The financial sector institutions do not get involved in setting up Community Development Programmes. In their case, whatever assistance they wish to provide to weaker sections of the community, it is given by way of instrumentality of lower interest rates. For example, the differential rate scheme, which the banks have to undertake at the behest of government, provides funding support to weaker section families at a rate which is considerably lower than normal interest rates. Some banks, however, do provide direct grants for certain specific purposes – say, for example, provision of scholarships to needy students belonging to Scheduled Castes category. Usually schemes of this type are restricted to certain selected districts – in most cases the lead districts of that very bank which is providing the funding support for specified causes.

As a result of initiative taken by a non-governmental organisation named Consumer Coordination Council, 24 commercial banks and 6 insurance companies prepared 'citizen's charter' whose main objective was to improve customer service. However, an evaluation survey undertaken by a non-governmental organisation had indicated that the awareness of citizen's charter was largely confined to senior executives of banks; and the staff and other employees, including those at the desk level, had no knowledge about even the existence of the charter.

Ethical codes or for that matter citizen's charters have a meaning only if they are implemented by financial institutions, with a measure of sincerity and thoroughness. These codes are not mandatory and it is for each individual unit to decide whether to adopt the norms or just hang them on the wall for display only and pursue the 'business as usual' path.

The slogan of 'Ethics is good business' is a well designed one and there is truth in this maxim. A businessman who earns the image of an honest and upright dealer does not have to look for customers, the latter themselves like to deal with him. Thus, honesty and pursuance of ethical standards can fetch good dividend to that businessman, who has earned a good image as an honest dealer.

It is a great pity that efforts put in by business in the form of Community Development and Social Welfare Programmes as also by way of compliance with ethical codes have so far not been commensurate with the economic status that this sector enjoys in the community. The number of companies that have set up these programmes is believed to be woefully small. One only hopes that those who actually manage these programmes are professionally competent and plan the activities in a scientific manner so that wastage of funds is avoided.

It appears that full significance of citizenship obligations, as defined in the Constitution, is either not understood fully by business or that it is not adequately aware of the constitutional provision relating to Fundamental Duties.

## III. Constitutional Values and their Relationship with Citizenship Obligations

The fact that the public awareness regarding Fundamental Duties has all these years been low has indeed the biggest stumbling block in operationalising the values and ideals enshrined in Article 51A of the Constitution. There are several reasons for the lack of public attention on Fundamental Duties. For one thing, it was not in the Constitution as originally enacted and was incorporated into it in November 1976 as part of the forty-second amendment. The logic behind the introduction of new Article 51A in the Constitution, as argued in the Swaran Singh Committee Report, was that fundamental freedoms as guaranteed by Fundamental Rights and the kind of socio-economic order as visualised in the Directive Principles would be achievable only if citizens do recognize their own duties towards the state as also towards fellow citizens. This logic did have a great deal of significance. Yet, the fact remains that Article 51A was introduced at a time when at the political level some other issues had led to a bitter controversy. The emerging environment at that time was thus by no means a propitious one.

Fundamental Duties as they now exist in the Constitution are not enforceable by courts. In the public mind a mistaken notion thus did exist, and to some extent does continue to exist, that a provision, which is not enforceable by law and which, therefore, is not going to attract, in the event of violation, any punishment as such is harmless and not worthy of great concern. Then, again neither Government nor Parliament did make any serious efforts to popularize the implications of Fundamental Duties. Among the non-governmental organisations also, not much attention was devoted to this subject for almost a decade after its incorporation into the Constitution. It was in 1986 that Citizenship Development Society (CDS), a non-governmental organisation undertook a couple of studies on Fundamental Duties and thereafter organised a Seminar in Delhi. A year later, it again organised another National Seminar on July 4 and 5, 1987 at Bangalore in collaboration with Gokhale Institute of Public Affairs. At the end of the Seminar a Declaration entitled 'Banglore Declaration on Citizenship Development and Fundamental Duties' was issued. The Text of the Declaration will be found in Annexure. Since then CDS has been relentlessly working to propagate the ideals of good citizenship. An extremely valuable contribution that CDS has made is a wonderful book entitled "Citizens and the Constitution" written by Dr. Subhash C. Kashyap, former Secretary General, Lok Sabha. It is a masterly document and has been discussed in a variety of forums, including at a symposium organised by CDS in collaboration with India International Centre, Dharam Hinduja International Centre of Indic Research and Rashtriya Jagriti Sansthan on 2 March, 1998 at New Delhi.

## IV. Fundamental Duties: A Natural Corollary of the Preamble and Parts III & IV of the Constitution

The Preamble is a masterpiece in brevity and concurrently in comprehensiveness. As the saying goes, it captures in a small vessel the vastness of an ocean. It enumerates essential features and values of the Constitution on which citizens of India had resolved to build the superstructure of India's sovereign Socialist Secular Democratic Republic. In terms of this resolve, it is the duty of each and every Indian citizen to ensure, through his/her actions and through vigilance on his/her part, that the kind of Nation that the Preamble has defined, does indeed emerge and continues to remain so. The Preamble then goes on to define certain ideals that citizens should, all the time, keep in the forefront and should strive to promote the ideals of Justice, Liberty, Equality and Fraternity. It is thus the duty of each and every citizen to work for the promotion of these ideals and to pursue them in his/her daily conduct.

Part III of the Constitution deals with Fundamental Rights of citizens and others. Main groups of Rights are:

1. Right to Equality (Articles 14 to 18)
2. Right to Freedom (Articles 19 to 22)
3. Right Against Exploitation (Articles 23 to 24)
4. Right to Freedom of Religion (Articles 25 to 30)
5. Cultural and Educational Rights (Articles 29 to 30) and
6. Right to Constitutional Remedies (Articles 32)

These are in the nature of elaboration of the values set out in the Preamble, in particular those relating to Justice (social, economic and political), Liberty (of thought, expression, belief, faith and worship) and Equality (of status and opportunity).

It is the bounden duty of the state to safeguard each of the rights and to ensure that the spirit behind them is duly and sincerely translated into action. Basically, they represent duties of the State. However, as one examines them closely, one would find that in the case of various articles of Fundamental Rights, an element of duty on the part of citizens also exists. This is illustrated by citing the following examples:-

- Article 15 (a) – Prohibition of discrimination on grounds of religion, race, caste, sex or place of birth: apart from the State following a policy that would prohibit any discrimination, it is the duty of each and every citizen also not to practise discrimination in his/her own conduct.
- Article 17 – Abolition of untouchability: It is the duty of each and every citizen not to practise untouchability.
- Article 18 – Abolition of titles: It is the duty of each and every citizen not to accept titles conferred by foreign states without obtaining permission from appropriate Indian authorities.
- Article 23 – Prohibition of traffic in human beings and forced labour: It is the duty of each and every citizen not to act in contravention of this article.

Part IV of the Constitution deals with Directive Principles of State Policy. Unlike Fundamental Rights, Directive Principles are not enforceable by courts. The principles indicated therein are nevertheless fundamental in the governance of the country. It is the duty of the State, albeit not enforceable by courts, to pursue policies and programmes in line with the principles indicated in this part of the Constitution. One may ask: Where and how do the citizens come into it? Citizens have a right to expect that the State will devise appropriate policies and programmes to implement the ideals set out in these principles. Concurrently, citizens have a duty too; a duty towards the State to give to the latter all co-operation and support in its endeavour to implement effectively the Directive Principles.

The citizen's duties discussed above are in the nature of derived duties as they indirectly flow from the Preamble, Fundamental Rights and Directive Principles. In contrast to them, there are specifically stated duties also which are contained in Article 51A of the Constitution and are termed as Fundamental Duties. They were inducted into the Constitution some 27 years after the initial enactment of the Constitution in 1949, the reason being that experience of the working of the Constitution during that period had shown that unless citizens themselves recognised their own responsibility in respect of the implementation of Fundamental Rights and Directive Principles, the kind of socio-economic milieu that the country was aiming to achieve would never materialize. Thus Fundamental Duties were conceived as a natural corollary of the provisions regarding Fundamental Rights and Directive Principles. It was indeed as well that it was done for the simple reason that collectively Fundamental Duties and derived duties taken together now constitute a fairly realistic and forceful charter of duties, covering all angles of citizen's constitutional obligations.

**Fundamental Duties as set out in the Constitution can be grouped under four broad categories indicated below:**

- **Duties of patriotic character;**
- **Duties requiring citizens to pursue noble ideals in their social behaviour;**
- **Citizens to protect and improve environment; and**
- **Citizens to adopt development oriented outlook.**

Category I above covers clauses (a), (c), (d), and (i) of Article 51A.

- Out of these and indeed out of all the clauses, that part of clause (a) which asks the citizens to abide by the constitutional ideals is indeed the most far-reaching one. Its implication is that citizens have to pursue not only all the duties that are listed in Article 51A but also the derived duties flowing from the Preamble, Fundamental Rights and Directive Principles. In addition to this it also asks citizens to respect the National Flag and the National Anthem. Both the Flag and the National Anthem are not mere symbols. They are much more than that; they represent sovereignty, honour, ideals and values that the nation has committed itself to protect and respect.
- Clause (c) is mainly designed to remind citizens that the Preamble of the Constitution contains resolve made by citizens that India shall be a Sovereign State meaning thereby that sovereignty – the supreme power – shall be with the citizens themselves and that they shall secure for the community Justice, Liberty, Equality and Fraternity assuring the dignity of individual and the unity and integrity of the Nation.
- Clause (d) asks the citizens that in case of war or external aggression citizens of the country should be prepared to respond to calls made by the community for defense.
- Clause (i) refers to two basic obligations and asks citizens to honour them. One: they should abjure violence and pursue the path of non-violence. Gandhiji pursued this path and preached this noble precept all his life. There is great truth in this precept. Non-violence does not mean achieving the objective by cowardice or unwarranted submission and surrender: it implies achieving the objective by

reasoning and persuasion. The second point made in clause (i) is safeguarding of public property. A patriotic citizen should honour this duty to the best of one's abilities

Category (iii) above covers three clauses of Articles 51A, these being clauses (b), (e) and (f).

In clause (b) citizens are asked to cherish and follow noble ideals which inspired the national struggle for freedom. Citizens are thus reminded about the spirit of selflessness and sacrifice that inspired freedom fighters. Their moral fibre was of a different kind. Non-violence was the guiding motto for them and ultimately India won the freedom struggle and what is even more important is that immediately after the second world war, several other countries, ruled by colonial powers, also achieved their independence.

Clause (e) asks citizens to promote harmony and spirit of common brotherhood amongst all the people transcending religions, linguistic, regional or sectinal diversities and renounce practices derogatory to the dignity of women. India is a pluralist society in which there are diversities in matters such as language, food habits, religions, etc. Despite these diversities there is fundamental unity in the country and the result is that India is one of the countries which is known to be a genuinely secular republic. Another point referred to in clause (e) asks citizens to abjure gender discrimination and ensure that women are treated properly and with dignity.

Clause (f) asks citizens to value and preserve the rich heritage of India's composite culture. India's culture has always accorded the highest rating to moral values. A society which has been in existence for almost five thousand years has rich and composite heritage. The point emphasised in this clause is that citizens of today must treat past heritage as an invaluable treasure.

Category (iii) deals with clause (g) of Article 51A. Citizens are asked in this clause to protect and improve natural environment, including forests, lakes, rivers and wild life and to have compassion for living creatures. There is no doubt of all that if degradation at environment continues to take place at the level at which it currently is, the coming generation will face a grim battle for getting to take steps to stop further degradation.

Category (iv) covers two clauses: clause (h) and clause (i).

Clause (h) asks citizens to develop scientific temper, humanism and spirit of inquiry and reform. In today's world, technology is changing fast and if India has to keep its head high and attain an appropriate position in the comity of nations, its citizens then have to develop scientific temper.

Clause (j) in a sense reiterates the same point as in clause (h) viz. modern-day Indian citizen should strive to achieve excellence in all spheres of individual and collective activity so that the nation constantly rises to higher levels of endeavours and achievement.

Clauses of Fundamental Duties discussed above cover a wide spectrum of moral and ethical values and obligations, important ones being developing patriotic fervour and love for one's own country; sincere adherence to duty with a sense of devotion and commitment; inculcating noble ideals of courage, sacrifice, selflessness and single-minded adherence to truthfulness and fair means; tolerance and openness to views of others; appreciation of India's culture and heritage; promotion of national integration and unity; concern for environment and wild-life; abjuring violence; promotion of equality, secularism and common brotherhood; developing scientific outlook, humanism and the spirit of inquiry and striving to achieve excellence all along the line. These are all inter-connected values and every citizen owes it to the community to pursue them with sincerity and imbibe them to the best of one's own capabilities.

Is each one of the duties and values flowing from Article 51A relevant to business? The answer is "yes", with the reservation that some may well be more relevant at a given time and for given segments of the society than others. In other words, at the operationalising stage, practical considerations may well suggest a measure of prioritisation but the long term objective should be inculcation of all the values by every citizen of the country, including those engaged in business.

## V. Steps for Operationalisation

### Essential elements of action plan:

For speeding up and strengthening of the operationalisation process, it is necessary for a business unit to work out a strategic plan, essential elements there of being the following:

(a) Internalisation of the concept of Fundamental Duties against the perspective of constitutional values and culture,

(b) Education and training and possible role of management schools in this regard, and

(c) Role of chambers and industry associations in helping business sector in the task of operationalisation.

### Awareness Gap

In an earlier part of this paper it has been stated that the lack of public awareness regarding constitutional values and obligations has been the biggest stumbling block in operationalising the values and ideals enshrined in the Constitution and that systematic efforts are called for to alleviate the situation in this regard. Rights and Duties are inseparable from each other. Fundamental Rights do confer rights on citizens but from them flow citizen's duties also. In a way, the same is the case with Directive Principles. Similarly from Fundamental Duties flow certain values and obligations. Thus, there is a logical linkage between the

Preamble and Parts II to IVA of the Constitution. One gets the true meaning of constitutional values only when one looks at them as a composite charter of obligations and values. This is the correct way of looking at Fundamental Duties and it is necessary that adequate public awareness is created in this respect.

**Internalisation**

There is a saying that charity begins at home. This can be modified to state that the task of covering the awareness gap should begin at home. In a typical business unit – ranging from small scale units to mega size corporations – one can identify three layers of core functionaries:

(a) top leadership,

(b) medium scale executives, and

(c) other employees including workers at the floor level.

The role of top leadership is crucial in making a business unit a success – measured not merely in terms of profit and loss account and balance sheet but also in terms of quality, industrial harmony, unit's image and also social performance. The top leadership by its dexterous handling of the functionaries in the other two layers would usually be in a position to influence the latter, particularly in matters such as social action field. By virtue of its long experience in business and interaction at top level with other segments of the society, the top leadership of a unit, in all likehood, may well be aware of the constitutional ideals and values and thus it can play an adequate role in spreading the message of constitutional values within the unit, easily and effectively. Once the process of internalisation of constitutional values has been completed then the process of application of those values to business operations would also become easy.

## Community Development and Social Welfare Programmes:

Some business units have already been making a measure of contribution by serving the community, taking up Community Development and Social Welfare Programmes and making an effort at implementing ethical codes in business dealings. However, as mentioned earlier, in both these areas, the effort put in so far by the business sector as a whole is in the nature of merely scratching the surface. A single sparrow does not make a spring. This should not be taken to mean that no one is making a worthwhile contribution. There are some business houses and corporations which are sincerely doing something on their own for the upliftment of the weaker sections of the community by taking up these activities but their number is woefully small. Hence as one looks at the business sector, one does come to a disappointing conclusion. There is need for enlightened business leaders to do some hard thinking about this state of affairs and step up activities by way of greater involvement in community development and social welfare programmes. In this context, it will be useful to get a directory (or more than one directory) compiled, giving an account of the activities taken up by business units in this regard. It is suggested that the task of compiling the directories should be undertaken by three national Chambers of Commerce – FICCI, ASSOCHAM and CII. They are in a position to request assistance of Regional and other chambers in the task of compiling directory/ies. The biggest advantage of such a directory would be that it would generate enthusiasm among others to set up similar projects and programmes and thus the activity by way of setting up new projects and programmes would get a boost.

## Codes of Conduct

Norms incorporated in existing codes of conduct formulated by chambers and other similar organisations happen to be restricted in contents in the sense that quite many constitutional values and obligations do not figure at all in the existing codes. One gets the impression as if authors of codes are not even aware of ethical values and obligations enshrined in Article 51A. This paper indicates in a summary form the contents of constitutional values and obligations. A comparison of those with chambers' existing codes would show that the latter are deficient in several respects. It is suggested that chambers and industry associations should have a re-look at their existing codes and then come out with model ones which can be the basis for formulating suitable codes, duly taking into account constitutional values on one hand and locational and such other considerations as nature of activity and kind of products or services which are predominantly covered by a chamber on the other. The formulation of appropriate codes is not the end of the journey. The journey would be deemed to have started only when the authors of the codes and their constituents comply with them in both belief and deed.

## Prioritisation in Respect of Fundamental Duties

As mentioned earlier, the ideal situation would be one in which each and every one in India has reached a stage at which everyone is fully conversant with values enshrined in the clauses of Article 51A and does indeed adhere to each one of them in one's actions. This is, however, an extreme position and may not be practicable, or even necessary, in actual life. What may serve the purpose is a system of prioritisation of obligations and values as contained in clauses of Fundamental Duties, the criterion for prioritisation being relevance of selected obligations, values to the nature of activity that the sector is engaged in. Applying this proposition, clauses (j) and (h) would be the ones which would be most relevant for business sector: clause (j) requiring citizens to strive to achieve excellence in all spheres of individual and collective activity so that the nation constantly rises to higher levels of endeavour and achievement. So far as clause (h) is concerned, the citizens are asked to develop scientific temper, humanism and the spirit of inquiry and reform. It should be the endeavour of business to pursue tasks assigned in these two clauses with sincerity and commitment, so that on the one hand the rate of technological development may get accelerated and on the other the urge for excellence may enable the Nation to scale new heights. In addition to clauses (j) and (h), clause (g) has also a measure of relevance to business. This clause calls upon citizens to protect and improve the natural environment. Business sector should play its due role in this field also.

## Education, Training and Possible Role of Management Schools

Education and training are important inputs for creating awareness in the community regarding Constitutional Rights, Duties and Values. The preceding chapters have dealt with, at length, relevant issues relating to value education which would cover inter alia constitutional values and obligations also. For those engaged in business, the appropriate media for imparting values and issues connected with value education would be discussion groups, seminars and workshops. It would also be desirable to tap the expertise of institutions like management schools and similar institutions in this regard.

## Role of Chambers and Industry Associations

Chambers of commerce and industry associations are formal spokesmen of business. There are several issues which individual business units may not be able to sort out on their own. Herein comes the importance of representative institutions of business viz. chambers and associations. They should give a lead to their members and use their initiative for organising conferences, seminars and workshops wherein the focus of discussion would be constitutional values and obligations.

## Notes

1. The same code would be applicable to officers and employees of administrative ministries concerned with public sector enterprises.
2. The term employees may be taken to mean C.E.O., executives and other employees of Public Sector Enterprises.

# 8

# Media and Citizenship Duties

*Prem Kumar*

## Constitutional Goals

The Constitution of India is the supreme law of the land. We, the people of this country, gave this Constitution to ourselves after we became free from foreign yoke. It is not only our fundamental law but also a charter of our social, political, economic and cultural values. The Constitution incorporates enforceable Fundamental Rights. It also contains all social and economic Human Rights as Directive Principles of State Policy and makes them fundamental in the governance of the country. Articles 36 to 51 of the Constitution give a blue print for the welfare of the State. These articles, inter alia, aim at securing a social order, promoting equality of sexes, organising democratic local government, providing a uniform system of laws, promoting education, health and a reasonable standard of living.

## Freedom of Speech

Article 19 of the Constitution of India guarantees various civil rights to the citizens of this country. These are common law rights and are recognised and guaranteed as the natural rights fundamental in nature. Article 19 (1) (a) of our Constitution guarantees to all the citizens the right to freedom of speech and expression.

## Media's Freedom

Media which includes television, radio and the press is one of the most effective means of mass communication in creating public opinion and also in arousing popular conscience. It is watched by people of all places in the country. It is a great instrument for public good and can be a public curse if directed to anti-social objectives. It has played a vital rôle in our national life. Inspite of creeping commercialisation, it has by and large maintained its concern for public interest. Although most of the media is in private hands, it is performing vital public functions. The freedom of the media is a species of the larger right of free speech and expression. Article 19 of 'A Universal Declaration of Human Rights' which has laid down essential freedoms that mankind should enjoy provides: "Everyone has the right to freedom of opinion and expression, the right includes freedom to hold opinion without interference and to seek, to receive and impart information and ideas through any media regardless of frontiers". Several rights emanate from this article like: (a) the right to seek and receive information and ideas from within the country and from abroad, (b) the right to impart information and ideas from within the country and abroad, (c) the right to seek and receive information and to impart information and ideas through any media whether print or electronic, (d) the right to form and hold opinion on the basis of information and ideas received from within the country or from abroad, and (e) the right to do so without any interference.

Freedom of communication involves two aspects, one 'the right to know' and the other 'the right to communicate'. In propagating the knowledge about these, the journalists, the press and the media in general have a vital role to play. They are the watchdogs of the rights. The communication could be made through any medium, newspapers or movies. Because of such wide impact on the society, the media should become conscious of the satisfactory discharge of its constitutional obligations.

It is clear that the idea of Human Rights only makes sense if we acknowledge the duty of all people to respect it. Human relations are universally based on the existence of both rights and duties. This golden rule is incorporated in the Fundamental Principles for Humanity proposed by the Inter Action Council of the United Nations' draft – 'A Universal Declaration of Human Responsibilities'. Bearing in mind the Golden Rule, the media has to inculcate in the masses the sense of fulfilling their societal obligations; the media has to educate the people that freedom can never be exercised without limits. Unrestricted freedom poses grave dangers. Great social injustices have resulted from extreme economic freedom and capitalist greed.

## Media's Limitations

This freedom must be exercised with circumspection and care must be taken not to trench on the rights of other citizens or to jeopardize public interest. This right is subject to reasonable restrictions on the grounds set out under Article 19(2) of the Constitution. The reasonable limitations can be put in the interest of sovereignty and integrity of India, the security of the State, friendly relations with foreign States, public order, decency or morality or in relation to contempt of court, defamation or incitement to an offence. The media, when it is run as a business, is also subject to the restrictions which may be imposed by State on any business, under Article 19(6) of the Constitution. When both rights are claimed and exercised by the media viz. the right to free speech and expression and the right to business, it will be subject to both the sets of restrictions viz. those under Article 19(2) and 19(6). It is obvious that over the years there has been ascendancy of consumerism and eroticism in the mass media and decline of ethical values in public life. The media as a whole has, therefore, to clearly understand its responsibilities towards the society and the nation arising from its constitutional obligations. There is need for the mass media to be relevant and morally responsible to the society.

Mac Bride Report emphasises the following responsibilities:

- Contractual responsibility in relation to the media and their internal organisation,
- Social responsibility entailing obligations towards public opinion and society as a whole, and
- Responsibility towards the international community relating to respect of human values.

Talking of social responsibility, exposure of corruption, particularly in public sphere, is indeed a duty of the media. In the political sphere, it becomes the duty of the media to promote national unity and national integration. In matters of communal reporting, the media must observe restraint and reports must not fan communalism and should be directed towards promoting communal harmony. The media must deal with social and economic conditions of the country in the proper manner. The media should expose all social, religious and caste prejudices. The media must champion the cause of exploited sections of the people. Media should also inform the people of the economic condition in the country. It becomes the duty of the media to bring to the notice of the people inefficiency and corruption, if there be any, in the implementation of any such plans and projects or in the functioning of any public centre undertaking entrusted with the responsibility of the development and the growth of the economy of the country.

The rights and responsibilities are related to the role the media as an institution is called upon to play. The Fundamental Duties enshrined in the Constitution for the citizens would also mould the role of the media in the society. The traditional role ascribed to the media is to inform, educate and entertain the people, whatever the character of the society. Media is a power and like all powers, it can be used for constructive as well as destructive purposes. The role of media, print and electronic, to the extent it can provide support to the students and teaching community in particular and in educating the general citizenry needs to be exploited to create an impact on the minds of the citizens to nurture Fundamental Duties in their lives. Media on the other hand has to pay adequate attention to the primary problems of mass poverty and mass illiteracy and of strengthening the moral character and fibre of the society. The common masses have a right to be informed on all matters affecting their lives. The media wields very great influence on the minds of the people. When mass media act in concert to bring a topic before the nation, it gains importance regardless of its inherent significance, conversely, when the media reduces the importance of a topic by a casual and low keyed treatment, popular interest is not aroused. It is necessary that media makes sincere efforts to cover adequately subjects related to poverty, health, education, religion, environment, social and racial prejudices and exploitation of every kind, social, political and economic.

### Code of Conduct for the Media

This brings us to evolving a Code of Conduct for the media. The freedom the media enjoy is to be exercised in the interest of the society. Moreover, freedom implies responsibility, for, the abuse of freedom ultimately destroys the freedom itself. Even the use of freedom by media is no exception. Its capacity to guide or misguide the people is tremendous. At the same time the media is to make itself accountable to the people. There is thus the constitutional need for an independent and autonomous institution like the media council which should evolve a code of conduct or of ethics for the media. There is the Press Council of India. Several Media Organisations, advertising industry and professional bodies set suitable standards. Some countries have appointed ombudsman to monitor and deal internally with the transgressions of the ethics by various constituents of the media.

**Press Council of India**

The print media has to be sufficiently sensitive in fulfilling its public function. To ensure that the press is alive to its responsibility, the Parliament created a statutory Press Council of India. The Council has been established with the object of preserving the freedom of the press and of maintaining and improving the standards of newspapers and news agencies in the country. It is to further these objects the Council is required, among other things, to help newspapers and news agencies to maintain independence; to build up a code of conduct for newspapers, agencies and journalists in accordance with high professional standards, to ensure on their part the maintenance of high standards of public taste, to foster a due sense of the rights and responsibilities of citizenship and to foster the growth of a sense of responsibility and public service among all those engaged in the profession of journalism.

As a result, the press has not developed community accountability to increase its credibility with the public. The press has to act with responsibility and professionally in fulfilling its code of a public service institution sensitive to the duties enshrined in the Constitution both for themselves and for the masses as well. The Press Council will have to pay more attention to this aspect of its functions. There are Guidelines to Board of Film Censors, the Broadcasting Code governing All India Radio, the Programme Code and the Advertising Code for Cable Operators, the Code for Commercial Advertising on Doordarshan, the Code of Advertising Practice of Advertising Standards Council of India and Code of Ethics for Editors adopted by the Standing Committee of All India Newspaper Editors Conference. It is the duty of those engaged in the Media to get these Fundamental Duties incorporated in the respective codes, regulations or the guidelines in the first instance, and work in the direction of these becoming known and followed by all concerned.

## Duties Implicit in the Constitution

The Supreme Court had taken the view in 1970 itself that the Constitution contains rights as well as duties. In the case of *Chander Bhan vs the State of Mysore* AIR 1970 SC 2042, the court observed, "It is a fallacy to think that under our Constitution there are only rights and no duties. The provisions in Part IV enable the legislature to impose various duties on the citizens. There can be no doubt that framers of the Constitution did not feel the necessity of incorporating specifically the Fundamental Duties in the Constitution as they presumed that these would be covered under the basic values inherent in the Preamble to the Constitution of India. Moreover they thought that societal and national obligations of promoting harmony and secularism and preserving the rich heritage of the composite Indian culture were basic and inherent values to be practised by each and everyone. These have been a part of the Indian tradition, mythology, religions and practices. As such no need was felt to incorporate them specifically in the Constitution".

## The Fundamental Duties

The Fundamental Duties formally came to be incorporated in a new chapter IVA by the Constitution (Forty-second Amendment) Act, 1976. Article 51A contains Fundamental Duties which include among others, the duty to abide by the Constitution and to respect its ideals and institutions; to uphold and protect the sovereignty, unity and integrity of India; to promote harmony and spirit of common brotherhood amongst all the people of India transcending all barriers; to protect and improve natural environment; to value and preserve the rich heritage of our composite culture to develop scientific temper, humanism and the spirit of inquiry and reform; and to strive towards excellence in all spheres of individual and collective activity. These duties are in consonance with Article 29(1) of the Universal Declaration of Human Rights which says,

"Everyone has duties to the community in which alone the free and full development of his personality is possible".

The Fundamental Duties enumerated in Article 51A are addressed to every citizen of this country. He owes these duties to the state, the country and the nation. Although this article may be said to be providing fundamental duties to be performed by every citizen, these may actually be called the rights in the citizenry. The endurance of a democratic republic depends on inspiring individual responsibility. Although these duties are not justiciable, nonetheless these act as guidelines for citizens in regulating their conduct in public life. It is expected that the citizen should be his own monitor while exercising and enforcing his Fundamental Rights. Every citizen has to remember that he owes the duties specified in Article 51A to the State and that if he does not care for the duties he should not deserve the rights. In this regard, it is essential to remember the message of Mahatma Gandhi who said that all rights to be deserved and preserved come from duty of citizenship of the world. From his one fundamental statement, perhaps it is easy to define duties of man and woman and co-relate every right to some corresponding duty to be first performed. We cannot enjoy the fruits of democracy unless we fulfill the responsibilities that devolve upon us as citizens. When everyone has the same rights, their enforcement is possible only when others respect them. The duty to abide by the Constitution, for example, is to accept the social and political philosophy enshrined therein and the citizens in any walk of life would be duty bound to regulate their conduct in furtherance of constitutional goals of social engineering and nation-building. For example, every citizen is required to uphold the sovereignty and unity of the country. Be it a politician, media person, a professional or an ordinary citizen performing his work in any sphere of life, everyone is expected to mould his role not only as a responsible subject of the State but also as a citizen. The responsibility to accelerate the pace of improvement in the country lies on the shoulders of every citizen by contributing his bit in whichever position he is. In a democracy the people are sovereign. They are the real rulers. Those who are concerned with various government organs and public institutions have to act in the interest of the people in general. Every holder of public office has to also obey the constitutional mandate like any citizen. All enforcement agencies should follow in practice the Seven Principles of Public Life contained in the First Report of the UK's Committee on Standards in Public Life which are: selflessness, integrity, objectivity, accountability, openness, honesty and leadership. To achieve the constitutional goals, every citizen is required to contribute his mite. Citizens have to perform their duties in a manner that respects the rights of others, protects the interests of the community and strengthens the nation's will and capacity to develop its potential.

The need to imbibe Fundamental Duties in the citizens of the country has arisen because Fundamental Duties have remained dead letter in the Constitution. It has not come out to reach even the class of people who handle the Constitution. We have become vocal in enforcing Fundamental Rights given in the Constitution. We have become a rights-oriented society. Indian approach has never been of abandonment of one's duties or of non-adherence to the Fundamental Duties. Entitlement of rights is dependent upon performance of duties. This can be done only if Fundamental Duties are brought into their minds and living process through teaching and educating. Media has to play a major role in this so that a right balance between Rights and Duties may emerge.

The media which wields very great influence and is expected to influence the minds of the people must play its role properly and effectively. It has to be appreciated that the importance that the media may enjoy will largely and necessarily depend on the credibility of the media. It, therefore, becomes the duty of the media to feed the people with true and correct information. It becomes the duty of the media to deal with every aspect of the political situation and political activities. The media must inform the people of the happenings all over the world and it is not enough merely to report such events or use scandals in high societies as may have sensational ingredients. It becomes the duty of the media to report all political, social and economic developments in the country and also in far away places since all such events may affect the country and the life of the community. In imparting information the media must observe objectivity and should make every report true, faithful and accurate. The media must not underestimate the intelligence of the people or overestimate the information and must appreciate that the role of the media which is indeed very important may only continue to remain so, as long as the media enjoy credibility and the confidence of the readers, viewers and listeners.

### Strategies for Effective Implementation of Fundamental Duties

The foremost matter to be considered is how best the concept of Constitution, its ideals and institutions could be made known to the masses by the mass media. The spirit of the Constitution is respected in the expression 'We the people of India' in the preamble which has found a generic meaning imparting directions of citizen behaviour on the part of all concerned. The Constitution preserves Indian ethos and our cultural heritage by promising dignity of the individual.

Although the task relating to operationalisation of the teaching of Fundamental Duties is largely that of the State governments and the Central government, the obligation of the media in this regard is no less. The powerful impact of media has to be fully exploited to transmit messages on Fundamental Duties to all levels of the citizenry.

**Duty to Abide by the Constitution**

The first Fundamental Duty is to abide by the Constitution and respect its ideals and institutions, the National Flag and the National Anthem. The relevant features of our Constitution are Parliamentary democracy, federalism, separation of powers, socialism, democracy, judicial review, rule of law, justice, liberty, equality, fraternity, individual dignity and unity and integrity of the nation. It is an instrument of social engineering and nation-building. It is respect for the constitutional values that the media must aim at. The media have to educate the masses. Secondly, media have to act as a catalyst of social and economic change. Creation of citizenry conscious of citizenship values including their rights and duties committed to the principles embodied in our Constitution is a prerequisite to social advancement, economic development and political progress of our country. For the media will have to give prominent coverage to rural India as well. The amount of efforts invested in political crime or other juicy stuff is much more than developmental features. The fundamental development problems facing the country are: achieving a high rate of economic growth, establishing a sense of legitimacy towards constitutional values and public institutions and creation of a sense of nationality among the diverse segments and layers of the society. It is true that these developmental problems cannot be solved by the mass media. But it is also true that these cannot be solved without the help of mass media. Solution of these problems would depend upon social mobilisation. The media has to create awareness. The developmental aim of improving the standards of living and the quality of life can be achieved only by liberating ingenuity and initiative in all the citizens of the country so that they can find new ways of doing things more quickly and more efficiently instead of repeating their activities in a routinised way. The media should lead the masses to the constructive path. This involves that each person must clarify his own goals and values and visualize his place in the future social pattern. This is the right and responsibility of a citizen in a free society. It also involves the policy decision of the group as a whole.

It has to be realised that the endurance of our republic depends on inspiring individual responsibility. Our country's future depends on the capacity of our people for self-governance. The media will have to play an important role in preparing the younger generations, in particular, for assuming their roles as constructive and responsible citizens. India is only as strong as the character and will of the people who comprise it. The Constitution cannot work in a society devoid of virtues. Our Constitution is a living document and the Media have to play duty of not only themselves abiding by it but also giving message to the people of the country coming from all walks of life of constitutional supremacy. Therefore, there is need to make a conscious effort by the media to promote an awareness of the constitutional obligations among the citizens. Media have also to act as a watchdog to see that those who man the Legislature, the Executive and the Judiciary and various other public institutions and instrumentalities of the State do not misuse the same. Convenience or expediency is not a measure of constitutionality. Constitution would live as long as constitutional structure vested in various organs is protected and preserved. There can be no doubt that virtue is the bedrock of constitutional democracy.

## The National Flag

Love for one's own country is inborn in all civilised men. It is manifested inter alia in respect to the national symbols and in identifying oneself with national pride and glory. One such symbol of sovereignty, national integration and pride is the National Flag. The Flag symbolizes the evolution of people's aspirations. On the eve of independence of India, the Tricolour (Tiranga) was adopted in the Constituent Assembly on 22 July, 1947.

Our flag represents the spirit of the nation, the tradition of synthesis which has characterised us for thousands of years. The emblem on the flag is an exact reproduction of the wheel from the capital of Ashoka's Sarnath Pillar which is a symbol of India's ancient culture. It is a symbol of the many things that India has stood for through the ages. It is a symbol of progress. It is a flag of freedom for all people. As Ms. Sarojini Naidu said at that time, under this flag, there is no difference between a prince and a peasant, between the rich and the poor, between man and woman. Dr. S. Radhakrishnan said at that time that the Ashoka wheel in the centre of the white is the wheel of law of Dharma. Truth or satya, dharma or virtue ought to be the controlling principles of all those who work under this flag.

Such are the significations of our National Flag, the tricolour. It is one of the fundamental duties of every citizen to respect the National Flag. The media have a duty to educate the masses about what Tricolour epitomizes and to encourage them to emulate the message it seeks to convey. And to accord due respect to this solemn symbol of the nation, the Flag Code provides various guidelines. It is the bounden duty of the media to educate citizens about the Flag Code and to familiarize them with the courtesies and ceremonies connected with it. Wherever the National Flag is flown, it should occupy the position of honour. It must not to be misused in any way. The misuse or improper use of the National Flag is obviously likely to offend the sentiments of the people. The media must educate people that whoever in public place or in any other place within public view burns, mutilates, destroys, tramples upon or otherwise brings into contempt (whether by words either spoken or written or by acts) the National Flag or any part thereof, is liable to be punished under the Prevention of Insults to National Honour Act, 1971. Media should also highlight the fact that its use for any trade, business, calling or profession or in the title of any patent or in any trademark or design without the prior permission of the central government is an offence under the Emblems and Names (Prevention of Improper Use) Act, 1950. Media have to devote sufficient attention to inculcating a sense of duty in the ordinary citizen to respect the National Flag which is essentially the State's instrument inseparably connected with nationality, sovereignty and national honour and pride.

The display of the National Flag by Indian people during sports meets including Asiads and Olympics displays their patriotic feelings and is public expression of their nationalism. The media should encourage people to show their love and respect for the solemn symbol.

The National Anthem and the Constitution are also considered the symbols of sovereignty and integrity of the nation. What applies to the case of Tricolour equally applies to Constitution. As regards National Anthem, no one is supposed to intentionally prevent its singing or cause disturbance to the assembly engaged in such singing. Anyone doing so can be punished upto three years or with fine or both. Media should, therefore, constantly educate people that Constitution and symbols of sovereignty could only be preserved by the public spirit and vigilance of its citizens and these could also be destroyed by its citizens.

**Role in Nation-Building**

Media can play a very effective role in nation-building. They can make the citizens cherish and follow the noble ideas which inspired our national struggle for freedom. They can inspire the citizens to defend the country and render national service when called upon to do so.

During the period of subjugation, the nationalists in India had a common goal viz. independence of the motherland. They followed different paths. Some were extremists, militants, religious extremists, mother worshippers, vendantists. Some advocated constructive nationalism. Some prepared the nation for freedom. There were also reformist movements like that of Brahma Samaj,

Arya Samaj, Ramkrishna Mission. There were moderates also. Then there were Congressmen. Aurbindo Ghosh was for an all-round development of Indian Nationalism. He emphasised that we are a nation inhabiting a great country in which many civilisations have met, full of rich material and unused capacities. We must cease to think and act like the inhabitants of an obscure and petty village. He was of the view that only by a general intellectual and spiritual awakening can this nation fulfill its destiny. He believed in the oneness of humanity. He was convinced that a spiritual awakening, a re-awakening to the true self of a nation was the most important condition of our national greatness. He believed that humanity was about to enlarge in scope by new knowledge, new power and capacities, which would create as great a revolution in human life as the physical science of nineteenth century. Here too, India held in her past, a little rusted and put out of use, the key of the humanity's future. Such was our ethos. The media must emphasize the noble ideals that our nationalists cherished and should work in consolidating the nation, raise its intellectual and moral tone, increase its economic efficiency.

As a first step the government has to prepare an adequate policy frame and mechanism for media towards nation-building. The media's potential has to be harnessed for issues such as rural development, empowerment of women, distance education, environmental protection, civic consciousness and human rights awareness. Media must be used as an important policy instrument in the social, educational and development planning and in fulfillment of constitutional goals of building a welfare society based on rule of law. The media policy must focus on mobilising human potential through (a) access to material resources like good health, education, housing, and (b) creation of a culture and environment that guarantees freedom, human rights and personal self respect. The nation-building process must centre around central values embodied in the preamble of the Constitution in the creation of a secular, socialist and democratic society.

As Media are both government-controlled and in Private sector, there is all the more need to not only formulate a comprehensive media policy but also create vital communication link within the government and between the government and the people in nation-building activities. There has to be a close co-ordination within the concerned government departments and other institutions responsible for implementation. The vast potential of the mass media has to be utilised for making different sections of the society conscious of their constitutional responsibilities and fundamental duties while integrating entertainment with socially relevant and useful message in the entertainment programmes themselves.

## Duty to Uphold and Project the Sovereignty, Unity and Integrity of India

Media have a special duty to uphold and protect the sovereignty, unity and integrity of India. Our constitutional values insist upon safeguarding sensitively and zealously our sovereignty. For media it means safeguarding people's democratic interests. The media must become alive to the dangers posed to our sovereignty by distortion of information and dissemination of news by certain market forces both within and outside the country because anti-national foreign forces may use extra-territorial news instruments to enter the country, install themselves with high-tech facilities and undo people's resistance when economic empires occupy critical areas. Once market economy, divorced from social good, becomes the dominant factor of media business, there is every chance of manipulation of mass response and mass culture to the detriment of public interest. Our values are apt to suffer eclipse if foreign domination of media committed to alien ethos, acculturation and political proselytisation, culminating in contempt for Indian heritage and constitutional basis romps in and once in, cannot be reined in. There will be subversion of our founding faith implicit in our Sovereign Socialist Secular Democratic Polity. It is, therefore, media's bounden duty to be on the guard and resist subversion for their very survival and the country's sovereignty. The Press Council of India which is a friendly watchdog of the press has to ensure that press remains free and responsible. One of the functions of the Council is to keep under review cases of assistance received by any newspaper or news agency in India from any foreign source. The Council has, therefore, to be vigilant in ensuring freedom of the press because a lapdog press, with strings pulled from abroad, is a threat to our independence. Sovereignty, integrity and fraternity, so important for national advance as an independent country, will be contingent upon the inner commitment of the media to their countrymen.

## Media's Duty to Promote Communal Harmony

It is the duty of the media to promote harmony and the spirit of common brotherhood amongst all the people of India transcending religious, linguistic and regional or sectional diversities. Communalism and casteism are most divisive maladies. The media enjoy which, the utmost freedom of expression, has a great and a vital role to play in educating and moulding public opinion on correct lines in regard to the need for friendly and harmonious relations between the various communities and religious groups forming the fabric of Indian political life and in mirroring the conscience of the best minds of the country to achieve national solidarity. The press should not indulge in the following which the Press Council of India considers as offending against the journalistic ethics in this regard:

(a) Distortion or exaggeration of facts or incidents in relation to communal matters or giving currency to unverified rumours, suspicions or inferences as if they were facts and base their comments on them;

(b) Employment of intemperate or unrestrained language in the presentation of news or views, even as a piece of literary flourish or for the purpose of rhetoric or emphasis;

(c) Encouraging or condoning violence even in the case of provocation as a means of obtaining redress of grievances whether the same be genuine or not;

(d) While it is the legitimate function of the press to draw attention to the genuine and legitimate grievances of any community with a view to having the same redressed by all peaceful, legal and legitimate means, it is improper and a breach of journalistic ethics to invent grievances, or to exaggerate real grievances, as these accentuate discord;

(e) Scurrilous and untrue attacks on communities, or individuals, particularly when this is accompanied by charges attributing misconduct to them as due to their being members of a particular community or caste;

(f) Falsely giving a communal colour to incidents which might occur in which members of different communities happen to be involved;

(g) Emphasising matters that are likely to produce communal hatred or ill-will, or fostering feelings of distrust between communities;

(h) Publishing alarming news which are in substance untrue or making provocative comments on such news or saying anything even otherwise calculated to embitter relations between different communities or regional or linguistic groups;

(i) Exaggerating actual happenings to achieve sensationalism and publication of news which adversely affect communal harmony with banner headlines or in distinctive types;

(j) Making disrespectful, derogatory or insulting remarks on or reference to the different religions or faiths or their founders.

**Media Programmes related to Culture and Values, and Environment: Clause (F) and (G) of Article 51A**

Media should make special effort to highlight programmes which support and promote activities related to national integration, culture and values, and environment. Ministries of the government have come out with various schemes/programmes related to these areas. These schemes/programmes have not caught the attention of the public. The concerned ministries allocate amounts to various NGOs to implement these schemes and programmes. The media will have to pay attention to the working and implementation of these schemes to see that the desired objectives of creating proper value system among the citizens are achieved.

The media should exercise considerable circumspection on the programmes, serials, pictures, news and advertisements affecting the morality or the decency of our people and cultural heritage of the country. The moral values in particular should not be allowed to be sacrificed in the guise of the social change or cultural assimilation. Our country has the distinction of giving birth to a galaxy of great sages and thinkers. The great sages and thinkers through their life and conduct provided principles for people to follow the path of right conduct. We have the concept of 'Dharma' (righteousness in every respect) a unique contribution of Indian Civilisation to the humanity of the world. It seems that unfortunately the foreign electronic media have been setting the agenda for the broadcasting system as a whole. Programming is increasingly determined by reach rather than by substance. Their central aim is the generation of revenue rather than the rejuvenation of cultural and social life. From the State monopoly we are shifting to 'market' monopoly where we are focusing attention on the consumer alone. Under genuine public control, it must perforce be the citizen. Instead of catering to the needs of the natural constituency which is the Indian citizenry, the media have indulged in political conformism, commercial aggrandizement and consumerism. This will necessarily entail programming which as a rule tends to debase tastes and lower standards. The Broadcasting system is deviating from the values and aspirations enshrined in the preamble of the Constitution, in its articles on the rights and duties of citizens and many of its directive principles – all of which taken together, constitute the conceptual basis of the Indian media.

The market is not a substitute for civil society. The Broadcasting System has to keep in mind the public interest and render public service. There is thus need for a strong and vibrant public broadcasting system in India. While our schools and colleges stuff more than mere information into the young, they impart no values to live by and thrive for. As a result, the vacuum in the educational institutions is being filled by the mammon of consumerism and eroticism in the mass media resulting in mis-education. The prime culprits are the various television channels and films. These are seducing the young, degrading public taste and deadening the social conscience through alluring advertisements and lewd or vivacious entertainment. The sexual intimacy including fantasy has been brought into public view for titillation. There is need for mass media to be relevant and morality responsible to the society.

We now come to the citizen's duty to protect and improve the natural environment including forests, lakes, rivers, wildlife and to have compassion for living creatures. The existence of mankind is threatened today due to pollution of air, water and earth and the ecological imbalance. This is due to over-population, over-cultivation, over industrialisation and urbanisation. The result is intensive and extensive exploitation of nature and congested, conditions. Further the use of dangerous technology for production and manufacture of poisonous products, the production of nuclear and chemical weapons, dumping of nuclear waste and the emission of green house gases that are prominent among the causes.

Due to the ever increasing population, the demand for land has increased and forest growth has been and is being cut down. Man has started encroaching upon nature and its assets. As a result, ecology and environment have been affected in a serious way. There is thus, need to be aware of its possible consequence. Much has not been done by the government in this regard, though courts have taken lead to ensure preservation of the environment and keeping the ecological balance unaffected. In it is not the task of the governments alone but the task that every citizen must undertake. It is a social obligation and fundamental duty of every citizen under Article 51A(g) of the Constitution which he has to be reminded by media as well. Media must spread awareness to citizens and arouse consciousness in citizenry for environmental protection. The media must highlight the privileges of the Forest Conservation Act, 1980 enacted with a view to check further deforestation. Any non-forest activity in a 'forest' area can be done only with prior approval of the central government. The State governments must promptly ensure total cessation of non-forest activity in 'forest' areas. Media should monitor whether directions of the courts in their various judgments are being followed or not. Reference may be made in particular to the judgment of Supreme Court in the case of *T.N. Godvarman Thirumulkpad vs Union of India and others,* where exhaustive instructions were given to the various State governments for the constitution of Expert Committees and for follow up action. Reference may also be made to the judgment in the case of *Vellore Citizens Welfare Forum vs Union of India and others,* where the central government was directed to constitute an authority under section 3 of the Environment (Protection) Act, 1986 to be headed by retired High Court Judge and other members having expertise in the field of pollution control and environment protection. This is with regard to the situation created by tanneries and other polluting industries in the State of Tamil Nadu.

It is the bounden duty of media to highlight the polluting factors and ecology-destructive activities and educate people to adopt alternative eco-friendly means. The media should also highlight the eco-friendly means of development in vogue in various fields. Further, the media have to strike at the root cause of the environmental destruction by preaching against consumerism.

Environment issues get too little space in the media. The media should take the role of an activist guard. It is not that it has to be a current topic or a part of political agenda that the media will pay attention to it. Media people have to remain alive to their constitutional responsibilities arising from Fundamental Duties to see that subjects like environment do not become a casualty. Media will have to train themselves to gain skill in presenting authentic available information in language everyone can understand. Media will have to remove the misconception that taking up issues of environment is acting anti-development.

Media can play a pivotal role in mobilising the people and making development participatory. Media can create public involvement through advocating and transferring knowledge, skills and techniques to the people. Media should play a more proactive role generating awareness about various rural development programmes.

## Duty to Safeguard Public Property and Abjure Violence

In a free democratic society, it is the duty of every citizen to safeguard public property and abjure violence. Various pressure groups, criminals, terrorists and anti-nationals indulge in destruction of public property and resort to violent methods to achieve their nefarious ends.

There is no doubt that protection of the people against most forms of violence is the first job of the governmental organisation: executive, legislative and judicial. The media have a duty to make people understand the varied manifestations of violence. In a democracy the violence of the ghetto, where common conditions include ignorance, deprivation, and official governmental failure to ensure that the laws are executed in letter and spirit is actually more than in the authoritarian state. Then there is a wide coverage of violence in films, TVs and cable programmes. Easy publicity on television has helped the spread of what might be called today's 'fashions' in adolescent violence, whether by students, minorities or other protestors. Media have a duty to avoid presenting acts of violence, armed robberies and terrorist activities in a manner that glorifies the perpetrators, acts, declarations or death in the eyes of the public. Acts of communal violence or vandalism should be reported in a manner as may not undermine the people's confidence in the law and order machinery of the State. Media should avoid writing about incidents in a style which is likely to inflame passions, aggravate the tension, or accentuate the strained relations between the communities/religious groups concerned, or which has a potential to exacerbate the trouble.

Media of any society are among the most important institutions. Democracy without free media is a contradiction in terms. Mass media should be the watchdog of democracy, and not the poodle of the establishment. Media have a greater responsibility today than they ever had to guide the nation and make every citizen conscious of his Fundamental Duties enshrined in the Constitution.

# PART III
# DOCUMENTS

# 9

# Bangalore Declaration on Citizenship Development and Fundamental Duties

Whereas participants in the National Seminar on Citizenship Development and Fundamental Duties held in Bangalore on 4 and 5 July, 1987 jointly sponsored by the Citizenship Society and the Gokhale Institute of Public Affairs, has deliberated in depth on the basic issues relating to Citizenship Development Society and Fundamental Duties in the aspirations of human kind and the conditions prevailing in India.

Whereas the Seminar is of the considered opinion that Citizenship Development and intrinsic awareness of Fundamental Duties at every level and in every station of life is essential for development and democracy, for freedom, peace and progress, and for justice and harmony.

## The Seminar Solemnly Declares

That development of good citizenship deserves to be accorded the highest priority in our national life and in a worldwide agenda for building up a more just, humane, peaceful and cooperative world order.

That citizenship development in India should be value based and should foster basic values enshrined in the Constitution of India.

That Citizenship Development alone can lead to a redefinition of the premises of power, a restructuring of the apparatus of power, a re-statement of national priorities, a reform of our public institutions and a meaningful and viable transformation of Indian Society.

That good citizenship is founded on an understanding and inculcation of the values of Human Rights and Human Obligations and on a civic culture of mutual consideration between citizens and state and among all groups of citizens and the instrumentalities of State.

That it is necessary to educate every person in each age-group and belonging to every vocation, trade and calling and in each and every station of life, including all echelons of leadership in every walk of life, in the duties and responsibilities of citizenship.

That citizenship education is vital to the equality of citizen participation, to the performance of representative functions in elective bodies and in professional bodies, trade unions, business associations and voluntary organisations.

That Education for Democracy and for good Citizenship for promoting and inculcating a sense of Fundamental Duties among Citizens and for reinforcing constructive vigilance should be undertaken on a countrywide basis as a continuing and ongoing programme for all age-groups.

That the concept and content of fundamental concerns and Fundamental Duties of Indian citizenship should be made on integral and intrinsic part of all curricular, extra-curricular and extension programmes of formal and non-formal education.

That there is need for a mass movement for citizenship development in India and for resurrecting, replenishing and reconstructing our liberal and humanitarian patriotism and sense of nationalism for advancing the twin causes of individual freedom and social justice.

That in every crisis and before every challenge faced by a developing democratic society such as India, an informed, enlightened, sensitive and self-respecting citizenry at all levels, committed to common national scale, working on the basis of mutual understanding, accommodation and consensus, and preserving a fundamental sense of integrity, fraternity and accountability is the most dependable human resource, the positive and constructive mobilisation of which alone will enable us to lay enduring foundations for future India.

That constitutional institutions of our democratic society and all those who are called upon by election, nomination or appointment to fulfil public responsibilities, the media, the intelligentsia, and the leadership in all walks of life and the entire body of Indian citizens should rededicate themselves to the ethos and the ideals of good citizenship, to the task of making those humanitarian ideals a pulsating and living reality of our national life, and to work ceaselessly for the realisation of those ideals through practical action programmes for the dissemination of citizenship values and norms, for vigilant, enlightened and meaningful, social audit of public participation, for the reform of our institutions and for an improvement in their working, for redress of public grievances and for optimising economic progress and social justice.

**And the Seminar Hereby Resolves**

That Citizenship Development Society should set up a Citizenship Training Centre to provide training facilities for upgrading the level of citizenship for persons in various walks of life and also undertake research studies bearing on citizenship developments;

That Citizenship Development Society should extend its activities to other states and regions, should play the role of an apex institution and for this purpose encourage the development of good citizenship values throughout the community and also provide facilities for affiliation with it of like-mined organisations; and

That Citizenship Development Society should also invite State Governments and other State and Local authorities to become its members and to lend support to its activities.

# 10

# Some Perceptions on Fundamental Duties

## Letter from the President, CDS to Chairman Committee on Fundamental Duties

Respected Vermaji,

I am grateful to you and your colleagues for so graciously inviting me to share my thoughts on Citizenship Development.

As I worked with my colleagues on the task entrusted by the Verma Committee to CDS to prepare a Handbook to facilitate Operationalisation and Teaching of Fundamental Duties, my mind was irresistibly drawn to the Dawn of India's Independence, to 15 Aug. 1947, when a new nation was born in an orgy of unprecedented communal violence, one country was partitioned amidst death and destruction on a massive scale and millions of innocent men and women fled in terror across the new boundaries to seek security in refuge. The first task was to rehabilitate the refugees, the second task was to integrate the Princely States into the new nation, the third task was to give ourselves the Constitution of India, and the fourth task was to plan and build an Independent India of our dreams. These tasks were carried out with smoothness and speed. The new polity, with a strong centre, vibrant federating units and parliamentary institutions soon took shape. The new economy with a judicious mix of private and public enterprise, of national planning and individual initiative of agriculture and industry was built up brick by brick. The New Society provided room for emerging social forces to overcome age-old obstacles and bring into being new institutions and mechanisms to develop science and technology and nourish our composite culture. In the international arena, India played a leading role in freeing the globe from the curse of colonialism, in initiating, sustaining and strengthening the Non-Alignment Movement and in the formation of Group Seventy Seven to secure modifications in the world economic order helpful to the economic development of newly independent nations.

This multi-dimensional effort at nation-building was led by the freedom fighters and carried out by thousands of individuals in all walks of life, who were driven by the national ethos based on the noble ideals which inspired the national struggle for freedom. No Handbook was required to teach them their duties and motivate them to play their role with diligence and determination. They did their part, I can testify from personal experience, naturally, without showing off, without song and dance, but with substantial impact. During the course of the first twenty five years of our independence, glorious heights were scaled in several areas of national endeavour. Our achievements were lauded at home and abroad. We were credited with having charted the course of democratic development.

But as we progressed down the Seventies, the first sign of fatigue began to appear on the horizon. Our national ethos seemed to be losing vigour and momentum. Its negative ingredients inherited from the colonial past began to raise their ugly heads. Sadly the rich diversity of our land tended to become a source of divisiveness. Fissiparous tendencies were strengthened by parties and politicians attempting to build vote banks on the bases of narrow caste groupings. As a result, growing cynicism about politics and declining respect for politicians disfigure our public life. Involvement of senior Civil Servants in nexus with corrupt politicians is eroding confidence in the integrity and impartiality of civil servants. The prevalence of corrupt practices at middle and lower levels, the general decline in behaviour patterns and in the conduct of mutual relations raise the cost of transactions, lower the efficiency of the economy and make it difficult for our goods and services to win in international competition.

The national scenario is distressing. The electoral campaigns for the thirteenth Lok Sabha have brought to the surface the distrust of the voter with the political process. The people are angry over persisting shortcomings in the provisions of basic services such as safe drinking water, health care, primary education and communications in the countryside. The new millennium will soon bring us interesting opportunities to make up deficits in democratic governance and international influence. The politicians cannot afford to indulge in the luxury of playing games in the coming weeks and months. A linear programme to teach and operationalize Fundamental Duties will by itself make no impact on the nation. Something wider, bigger and deeper is the need of the times.

The maladies which afflict our Polity have their origin in the failure over the preceding fifty years to provide for educating CITIZENS in democratic governance. Our Constitutions has made the individual citizen the fundamental unit of the Indian Polity. He is both the sovereign and subject at the same time. His or her ethos, value system and behavioral pattern, while acting in either capacity, as ruler or ruled, inevitably determines the quality of democratic governance and yet no systematic effort has been made so far to prepare the CITIZEN for the discharge of this great responsibility.

The hope for improving the quality of governance and

for resolving the myriad problems that confront us lies in the hands of the citizens, in their understanding the VALUES they must practise and the DUTIES they must discharge. The current conjuncture of social and economic forces and the disgust aroused by falling ethical standards provide a timely opportunity to launch a nation-wide Nav Nirman Movement with the aim of enabling all citizens to become aware of their rights and responsibilities under the Constitution and understand their obligations to observe constitutional values and carry out Fundamental Duties in their day to day activity. A responsible citizenry may be expected to develop the will and capacity to tackle basic problems at home and ensure that India occupies its rightful place abroad.

There is no dearth of literature from which the Aims and Objects of the proposed Movement may be derived. In his book entitled "Citizens and the Constitution". Dr. Subhash C. Kashyap has distilled from the provisions of the Constitution a Charter of some eleven democratic values. Article 51A of the constitution lays down in unambiguous language the ten (now eleven) duties each citizen is expected to carry out. Your Committee's Interim Report develops several valuable concepts in this regard. On the basis of available experience, it would not be difficult to prepare a statement of the Values and Duties which citizens are expected to observe in their day to day activity. Such statement must derive its authority from the Constitution. It must also command national consensus. Since the main OBJECTIVE is to transform the mind-sets of citizens, it will be appropriate to request the President to inaugurate the Movement.

A few words about the Organisation of the proposed Movement may be in order. Its leadership may be vested in a National Council for Citizenship Development. The Council's composition must be broad-based so as to reflect the diversity of the nation's citizenry, the council may elect a small Executive Committee to carry out mainly creative, coordinating and catalytic functions. While eschewing bureaucratisation of its administrative structure, the responsibility for field work must be fully decentralised. The practical task of generating awareness of citizenship values and facilitating their application at work places is best carried out by citizens themselves through the Departments in which they work and the institutions to which they belong.

The task of "operationalising" citizenship values is formidable and complex. There are wide variations in the conditions and characteristics of different segments of citizens. The eminent persons who worked on the Handbook found it convenient to divide the citizens in eight target groups. They looked at the group profile, identified the values particularly relevant to each group, discussed their application to live situations, and put forward suggestions for their operationalisation. Their work provides a useful base for initiating action programmes and holding workshops to evolve implementation strategies.

In building up good citizens for the future, our educational system has a very special responsibility. They must develop tools and techniques to ensure that the pattern of behaviour expected of a good citizen gets ingrained into the individual pupil and becomes a natural part of his or her personality. NCERT AND SCERT have taken initial steps in this regard. They should be mandated to make systematic efforts, develop course materials and devise effective curricular and extra-curricular programmes to secure that deliberate behaviour modification becomes an essential ingredient of the educational process. A great deal depends on the ingenuity and dedication of teachers. A nation-wide movement to train and honour teachers in inculcating citizenship values could bring about impressive transformation in the opening decades of the new millennium since University students constitute the most dynamic and progressive component of our body politic, the universities could play a crucial role by organising compulsory as well as optional programmes to enable student participants to become good citizens themselves and learn to discharge their obligations to the institutions to which they belong and to the community of citizens in general.

Elected functionaries and appointed Civil Servants have a major role to play in the proposed Movement. They have the same rights and duties as other fellow citizens. If they succeed in observing citizenship values while performing their tasks, they would also succeed in securing general improvement in the quality of life. Fortunately they are blessed with an impressive network of training and research institutions which can be easily harnessed to develop teaching modules and organize brain storming workshops in support of the effort to make citizenship values a living reality. Similarly, the process of degeneration in the Administration of Justice can be reversed if Law Colleges and Bar Associations succeed in organising teaching courses on the application of constitutional values to practical aspects of judicial procedures and legal practices.

A big contribution may be expected from the field of Business and Industry. Management schools should be willing to add to their curricula a paper on the application of constitutional values to the conduct of business. I trust Business Leaders and their organisations will find it profitable to take interest in internalising citizenship values and in ensuring that their observance becomes an indispensable ingredient of business ethos.

Media weilds immense power to influence public opinion and rouse individual consciousness. Its constituent bodies should be keen to help media to respect citizenship values and generate support for the Movement.

Citizenship Values as derived from the Constitution have a moral quality and an ethical dimension. The OBJECTIVE of the Movement is to ensure that these values become a part of our National Ethos and govern the conduct of all our citizens. It can best be achieved by the widest possible participation of the citizens themselves in the Movement.

I have taken advantage of your gracious invitation to give expression to my thoughts freely. Please forgive me if I have transgressed the boundaries of logic or relevance.

With very warm regards,

Sincerely yours

**(Dr. K.B. Lall)**

President, CDS

# 11

# Salient Recommendations of the Committee on Fundamental Duties of Citizens

## (a) Generating Awareness and Consciousness

Citizenship is a solemn duty which every individual must discharge with due diligence and dedication.

The current conjecture of social, economic and political forces calls for a movement which captures the imagination of masses and motivates all categories of citizens to abide by the provisions of the Constitution in performing their duties and exercising their rights.

Towards creating more awareness and consciousness of Fundamental Duties among citizens, the Committee recommends the following:

- Organising advocacy and sensitisation programmes;
- Preamble to the Constitution of India and the clauses of Article 51A on Fundamental Duties to be appropriately displayed on all government publications, diaries, calendars and at public places so that they always remain in the focus of the citizens.

- Radio and video spots, highlighting important messages related to Fundamental Duties, in the background of proper music and the National Flag, to be commissioned by All India Radio, Doordarshan, and other DD Channels. This should become a regular feature at least in all Doordarshan channels around the country, once or twice a day, to have significant impact over the years.
- January 3 to be observed as Fundamental Duties Day.
- Need to set up an autonomous body to act like ombudsman on Citizenship Values which could create a mechanism to act as a catalyst towards overseeing operationalisation of Fundamental Duties. The human resource of the senior citizens could be effectively utilised for discharging commitment of this nature. The financial implications for setting up this body which has also a state funding aspect will have to be taken into consideration.
- Small booklets on various aspects of Fundamental Duties written in a language easy to understand could also be developed for different levels of citizens. Such booklets should be particularly utilised by the citizens learning through Non-Formal Education (NFE) and adult Education (AE) Programmes run by state governments and voluntary agencies. The concept of Fundamental Duties can form a major component of NFE and AE programmes.
- The media should exercise considerable circumspection on the programmes, serials, pictures, news and advertisements affecting the morality or the decency of our people and cultural heritage of the country.
- Environment issues need to get more space in the media. The media should take the role of an activist guard. It is not that it has to be a current topic or a part of political agenda that the media will pay

attention to. Media people have to remain alive to their constitutional responsibilities arising from Fundamental Duties to see that subjects like environment do not become a casualty.

- Media have a duty to avoid presenting acts of violence, armed robberies and terrorist activities in a manner that glorifies the perpetrators' acts, declarations or death in the eyes of the public. Fundamental Duties are not only sacrosanct but also have the element of compulsion requiring obedience, provided the machinery of the state appreciates its true nature and motivates the implementation machinery towards this end. The primary need, therefore, is to ensure a faithful and effective implementation of the existing legislation in the area covered by legislation and for prompt measures to legislate in the remaining field to fill the legislative vacuum.

### (b) Optimising Benefits from Existing Schemes/ Programmes

Towards optimising benefits from the existing schemes/ programmes on national integration and communal harmony, culture and values, and environment, the Committee recommends the following:

- Need to further activate and monitor the work of the institutions and NGOs who are sanctioned these schemes by the concerned ministries of Home, Human Resource Development and Environment and Forests.
- While approving the financial assistance to the NGOs, the focus of their programmes must deal with aspects of national integration and communal harmony, culture and values, and environment which are in tune with the spirit of clauses (e), (f) and (g) of Article 51A. Definitive evaluation of the work done under the existing schemes/programmes would be

desirable, and the concerned Ministries/Agencies should take stock of the impact generated. If any mid-course corrections are called for, they should be incorporated forthwith.

### (c) Protection and Improvement of Environment

Towards protection and improvement of environment the Committee recommends the following:

- The Doctrine of Trust emphasises that there is no ownership in natural resources and that every generation should make judicious use of them, as trustee for the future generations. Coordination between all the law enforcement agencies is essential to achieve the desired results. The constitution of India lays emphasis on this aspects by enacting Article 48A as a Directive Principle of State Policy and Article 5IA (g) as a Fundamental Duty of every citizen.
- To enforce strict compliance of the various legal provisions in this regard as available in the directions of the Supreme Court of India on Article 51A. If the existing legislations are inadequate to enforce the needed discipline, such a legislative vacuum must be filled suitably to ensure enforceability.

### (d) Reorienting Approaches to School Curriculum

Any exercise in curricular analysis alone is bound to offer only fragmented view of educational processes in Fundamental Duties. The entire range of issues related to effective inputs that ensure appreciation, respect, value, etc. emerge out of instructional processes and schooling as a holistic experience. For this angle, it is necessary to review education in Fundamental Duties from the point of view of pedagogical and androgogical processes.

Towards reorienting approaches to school curriculum, the Committee recommends the following:

- There is a need for a fundamental transformation in the direction and approach to curricula for teaching Fundamental Duties in school and teacher education institutions. Citizenship values should be understood by all concerned as a combination of rights and duties. Appropriate steps in this regard need to be initiated through the educational process to achieve the desired results in the long run.
- Preamble to the Constitution of India and the Clauses of Article 51A of the Constitution on Fundamental Duties to be printed in all school textbooks, supplementary materials and general publications brought out by the NCERT and the school Textbook Bureaus in the States/Union Territtitory Administrations. There is a pedagogical significance of this approach. Increasing understanding of androgogy alongside pedagogy reveals that knowledge of goals itself is tool of learning. When students understand their obligations, they are likely to learn their own way fulfilling the obligations.
- Presentation of the values inherent in each clause of article 51A through anecdotal talks of morning assemblies in schools.
- Seminars, debates, competitions on different aspects related to Fundamental Duties to be made regular feature of the co-curricular activities of schools.
- In designing a programme of education on Fundamental Duties, there has to be a conscious effort to develop an instructional design that fits into a multi-channel learning environment.
- It is important to recognise that we are living in the multichannel learning environment where learning accrues from a large number of sources like home, school, community, print media, electronic mass media, knowledge networks, internet, etc. Given the

ever spreading tentacles of multichannel learning environment and increasing globalisation of mass media, the issue of education in Fundamental Duties, particularly as a school-dependent education, needs due consideration.

- The points of view mentioned under Major Issues in the Critique on School Curriculum are very relevant for reviewing of existing curricula and Planning for newer strategies of teaching of Fundamental Duties. These suggestions should be referred to the NCERT and the SCERTs and the State Textbook Bureaus for taking them into account while a curricular renewal exercise is undertaken by them. The basic question is whether Fundamental Duties as such need to be highlighted as an independent curricular area or its natural integration should be planned in various areas of curriculum as exercises in value orientation. The net goals of both the approaches are the same but the nature of emphasis certainly becomes different. The flexibility to experiment with either approach can be left to curriculum developers to experiment.
- Fundamental Duties across various primary and secondary classes should be provided in a spreadsheet which can be used to plan curricular coverage by mapping topics and themes from various subjects related to the clauses pertaining to Fundamental Duties. The curricular reorganisation, particularly in formulating textbooks, should be done on the basis of such a spreadsheet. It may not demand a serious change in the curricular content but may require alternative treatment relating the content to the relevant Fundamental Duties. Linked to this is the shift of focus from merely teaching the content of the Constitution to the process of education necessary to internalise the values inherent in it. Curricular

treatment of Fundamental Duties not only needs to cut across different subjects but should also increase in depth as one moves from one level of education to another.

**(e) Elimination of Gender Bias**

In order to ensure dignity of women, gender biases and sex-stereotyping must be eliminated from all school and colleges textbooks and this should be given as a mandate to all curriculum development agencies, both at national and state levels.

**(f) Reorienting Teacher Education Programmes**

It is not enough that the teachers are made aware of Fundamental Duties; it will also require educating them in communicating Fundamental Duties to the students and impressing on them the need to abide by the dictums of the same. For a serious business of education in Fundamental Duties at the school level, teachers of all subjects at all levels have to be oriented and trained. Accordingly, the curricular coverage to Fundamental Duties have to be deliberate and pre-designed.

It will be necessary to develop a blueprint indicating reflection of various clauses in various units and topics of various papers in teacher education curricula. Preparation of teachers through well designed teacher education programmes, would actually play a very significant role in ensuring understanding and internalising of Fundamental Duties in our schools and communities.

Towards reorienting teacher education which is the most crucial input in operationalising Fundamental Duties, the Committee recommends the following:

- A sensitisation module based on Fundamental Duties to be made an integral part of all teacher education programmes, organised by National, State and District level institutions. Large scale teacher orientation programmes should be planned on this theme.

- The NCERT, the NCTE, the NIEPA, and other institutions around the country should organise seminars in various parts of the country to familiarise the teachers with the strategies for operationalising the teaching of Fundamental Duties.
- An effective way to institutionalise the concept of Fundamental Duties in the teacher education is to incorporate it in the elementary and secondary pre-service teacher education curriculum. This should be supplemented by a suitable co-curricular programme, which should aim at offsetting some of the shortcomings in the curricular approach especially in terms of attitude and value development.
- In view of very little content on Fundamental Duties included in the elementary and secondary teacher education curricula, as revealed by the Critique, what is needed is a vigorous advocacy with state educational agencies, teacher education institutions and university departments of education for conscious inclusion of this component in the curricula.
- It should be possible for the NCTE with its status, of a statutory body to influence teacher education curricula in different universities in a more substantial way, with reference to teaching of Fundamental Duties.
- In order to overcome the disadvantage of fragmented treatment and discussion on Fundamental Duties, it is suggested that an independent comprehensive unit encompassing familiarisation with the Constitution of India and Fundamental Duties of citizens thereunder should be incorporated in elementary and secondary teacher education courses. In India, evaluation system influences the educational process specially the quality of class-room teaching

significantly, and as such as separate unit on Fundamental Duties ensures due importance and weightage to the concept in the class-room teaching.

- Considering the importance of upholding and protecting sovereignty, unity and integrity of India, it is felt that NCC should be made compulsory in all the pre-service teacher education institutions, both elementary and secondary.
- Fundamental Duties Week may be observed in all teacher education institutions every year. The objective of this Week may be to create essential awareness and positive environment for the inculcation of attitudes and values as reflected in Article 51A of the Constitution of India.
- A great deal depends on the ingenuity and dedication of teachers. A nationwide movement to train and honour primary school teachers as builders of citizens, if launched with sincerity and purpose, could bring about impressive transformation in the educational system.

**(g) Incorporating Fundamental Duties in Higher and Professional Education**

Towards incorporating Fundamental Duties in the courses and programmes of higher and professional education, the committee recommends the following:

- The current Human Right Education Initiative of UGC should be referred to as 'Human Rights and Fundamental Duties Education Initiative'.
- The UGC, while considering giving grant and support to proposals received from universities and colleges under its Human Rights Education Initiative for introducing Degree/ Diploma/ Certificate Courses and other programmes in Human Rights, may advise on incorporating Fundamental Duties as an essential

component of their respective proposals.

- Workshop on Devising curriculum, evolving teaching methodologies and orienting faculty to make Fundamental Duties consciousness as the central focus of educational experience should be seriously considered by the University system. The UGC could consider issuing necessary instructions in this regard to the institutions under its control.

**(h) People's Representatives from Panchayats to Parliament**

Towards the responsibilities of people's representative, the Committee recommends the following:

- Special efforts should be made to ensure that legislators are aware of the Fundamental Duties as the same are also their duties as citizens. This would mean that special programmes may be organised at the parliamentary and state assembly levels. The Corporation, Town Area Committees and the Panchayati Raj institutions should also be involved in this effort as they alone can take the appropriate messages down to the grass roots.
- Candidates seeking the mandate of the people must eschew arousing sectarian passions and take all practical steps to promote national unity and integrity.
- Elected Representatives should refrain from interfering in the functioning of governmental and non-governmental institutions. They should observe the laws themselves and help law enforcing agencies in dealing with law breakers.
- It should be the endeavour of Elected Representatives to organize/strengthen a network of activities to gather support for small family norm, to protect and improve natural environment, to safeguard public property and to abjure violence.

- Orientation programmes for new members of Parliament and State Legislatures need to be strengthened to provide an adequate measure of understanding of Fundamental Duties and their application to the work of Elected Representatives.

### (i) Public Administration and Civil Servants

It is the duty of every citizen to obey the constitutional mandate. Every holder of a public office has additional duties as a citizen besides the duties imposed by virtue of the office she/he holds. Sensitivity of all enforcement agencies is essential for realising the promise held out in the Constitution.

Strict observance of codes of professional ethics by professional bodies has to become important in this regard, and such bodies must design their own programmes which help oprationalisation of Fundamental Duties.

Towards the obligation of public administration and civil servants, the Committee recommends the following:

- Module on Fundamental Duties should be adopted for inclusion in the Courses of different Training Institutions connected with the training of civil servants.
- It should be the responsibility of the senior public servants to project the image of administration as people-friendly and responsive to the problems and sufferings of the citizens.
- The Government should move towards giving greater access to information. Transparency and free supply of information will reduce corruption and ensure accountability.
- Secretaries to Government, Managing Directors in the public sector, Heads of Departments, Heads of Offices/ Field Units should be made squarely and personally responsible for taking detailed measures

for rooting out corruption in their assigned areas of responsibility. A set of guideline could be supplied to them for strict compliance.

- There should be an in-built mechanism for handling cases of dereliction of duty by public servants where a public grievance has not been redressed with a stipulated time.

**(j) Administration of Justice**

Towards the Administration of justice, the Committee recommends the following:

- A Judicial Academy should be set up to provide facilities for continuing education of Judges, to focus their attention on Constitutional Values and Fundamental Duties, to foster constructive interaction between the Bar and the Bench and to facilitate application of modern techniques of management to the transaction of judicial business in the Courts.
- Bar Councils and their affiliated Bar Associations must share the responsibility for ensuring that their members not only appreciate the value of complying with Fundamental Duties but also strive to implement them while pursuing their professional work.

**(k) Business and Industry**

Towards the role of business and industry, the Committee recommends the following:

- Business Leaders, Business Organisations and Management Schools have vital roles to play in internalising basic values, in widening financial and technical support for community development programmes, and in ensuring that ethical codes become indispensable ingredients of business ethos.
- Business and Industry have obligation to perform the duties, both implicit and explicit, enjoined by the Constitution. However, in discharging social

responsibilities, only a small percentage of the Business Community has undertaken social welfare and development programmes. Important Chambers of Commerce and Industry Associations have taken initiative for formulating norms of ethical conduct for business dealings. But the action taken to secure compliance with the codes leaves much to be desired. This should be pursued more vigorously.

**(l) Media**

Media of any society are among the most important institutions. Democracy without free media is a contradiction in terms. Mass media should be the watchdog of democracy, and not the poodle of the establishment. Media have greater responsibility today than they ever had to guide the nation and make every citizen conscious of his /her Fundamental Duties enshrined in the Constitution.

- The powerful impact of media including electronic and print media has to be fully exploited to transmit messages on Fundamental Duties to all levels of citizenry.
- The fundamental development problems facing the country are: achieving a high rate of economic growth, establishing a sense of legitimacy towards constitutional values and public institutions and creation of a sense of nationality among the diverse segments and layers of the society. It is true that these developmental problems cannot be solved by the mass media. But it is also true that these cannot be solved without the help of mass media. Solution of these problems would depend upon social mobilisation. The media have to create awareness in this regard.
- There is need for the media to make conscious effort to promote an awareness of the constitutional obligations among the citizens. Media have also to

act as a watchdog to see that those who man the Legislature, the Executive and the Judiciary and various other public institutions and instrumentalities of the State do not misuse the same. Convenience or expediency is not a measure of constitutionality. Constitution would live as long as constitutional structure vested in various organs is protected and preserved. There can be no doubt that virtue is the bedrock of constitutional democracy.

- Media should constantly educate people that Constitution and the symbols of sovereignty could only be preserved by the public spirit and vigilance of its citizens and these could also be destroyed by its citizens.
- The potential of the media has to be harnessed for issue such as rural development, empowerment of women, distance education, environmental protection, civic consciousness and human rights awareness. Media must be used as an important policy instrument in the social, educational and development planning and in fulfillment of constitutional goals of building a welfare society based on the rule of law.
- As media are both Government controlled and in Private Sector, there is all the need to not only formulate a comprehensive media policy but also create vital communication link within the government and between the government and the people engaged in the nation-building activities.
- Once market economy, divorced from social good, becomes the dominant factor of media business, there is every chance of manipulation of mass response and mass culture to the detriment of public interest. Our values are apt to suffer eclipse if foreign domination of media committed to alien ethos, acculturation and political proselytisation, culminating in contempt for Indian heritage and

constitutional basis romps in and once in, it cannot be reined in. There will be subversion of our founding faith implicit in our Sovereign Socialist Secular Democratic Polity. It is, therefore, media's bounden duty to be on the guard and resist subversion for its very survival and the country's sovereignty.

- Media should make special effort to highlight programmes which support and promote activities related to national integration, culture and values, and environment.

# Bibliography


Ambasht, N.K., (1987), Role of primary teachers in national Integration and Nation Building, *Bhartiya Adhunik Shiksha*, 4 (3), 1+5.

Bandiste, D.D., (1999), *Humanist Values: A source book*. Delhi: B.R. Publishing Corporation.

Bahin, A.J., (1982). Value-oriented Education : Part IV, *The Progress of Education*, 57 (2), 26-30.

Bahin, A.J., (1982), Value-oriented Education : Part III, *The Progress of Education*, 57 (1), 2-7.

Balann, K., (1989), *Education for Excellence*, New Delhi : Intellectual, p. 87.

Barbosa, J.A.F., (1997), Interdependence : A Basic Assumption for the Building of Human Values, *Journal of Human Values*, 3 (1), 19-127.

Beg, M.H., (1985), *Impact of Secularism on Life and Law*, New Delhi, p. 36.

Budhananda, Swami, (1983), How to Build character : A Primer, New Delhi, Ramakrishna Mission.

Chinare, B., (1997), *Education and democracy*. New Delhi: APH, viii, p. 201.

Chatterjee, P.C., (1995), *Secular Values for Secular India*, New Delhi : Manohar Publishers.

Chittibabu, S.V., (1987), Value Orientation in Higher education, *University News*, 25 (42), 1-7.

Choudhary, N.R., (1989), Values and Value-oriented Education, *Journal of Indian Education*, 15 (1), 15-17.

Colaco, J.M., (1982), *Morals in Daily Life*, Book I–V, Madras: Samba Publishing Co.

Dass, B.R., (1982), Moral Science, Book I – VII, Madras : Saha Publishing Co. *Democracy and Education in India*. New Delhi : Deep and Deep Pub., pp. 202-12.

Dwivedi, K., (1987), Role of Education in National Integration. *Bhartiya Adhunik Shiksha* 4 (3) 14-16.

Edger, M., (1982), *Value and Curriculum, New Frontiers in Education*, 12 (3), 23-27, Education in Human Values, Ch. I & II Government of Karnataka (1987).

Gupta, N.L., (1999), *Neo-Humanism and Human Values*, New Delhi : Mohit publications.

Gupta, K.M., (1991), Value in Education, *Bhartiya Adhunik Shiksha*, 8 (4), 21-24.

Joshi, K., (1997), *Education for Character Development*, Delhi : Dharam Hinduja International Centre of India Research, p. 92.

Joshi, J.V., (1982), Problems in Moral-education, *The Progress of Education*, 57 (2), 31-34.

Joshi, J.V., (1982), Problems in Moral Education, *The Progress of Education*, 57 (5), 98-102.

Joshi, J.V., (1982), Moral Education : Approach and Perspective, *The Progress of Education*, 57 (3), 50-52.

Joshi, J.V., (1982), Techniques of Moral Education, *The Progress of Education*, 57 (6), 122-129.

Kashyap, Subhash, (1994), Basic Constitutional Values. Delhi : Ajanta, Kashyap, C. Subhash (Ed.), (1998), *Urgency of Value Education and Primacy of Girl Child*, National Agenda for Educational Reforms, Delhi, Uppal Publishing.

Kashyap, Subhash C. (1993), *Delinking Religion and Politics*, Delhi.

Kashyap, Subhash C., *Citizens and the Constitution*, CDS Publication.

Kareem, S.A., (1989), Education in Human Values, *University News*, 27(10).

Kundu R., Kundu N., (1983), The Domain of Value Assessment Techniques A Review, *Bombay Psychologist*, 5(1), 49-59.

Lobo, G., (1980), Some Issues in Moral Education, *New Frontiers Education*, 10(2), 79-96.

Mohanty, J., (1986), *Democracy and Education in India*, New Delhi : Deep and Deep Pub., pp. 202-12.

Mehrotra, R.C., & Arora, R.K., (Eds.) (1994). *Education, Science and Human Values*: Essays in Honour of Prof. D.S. Kothari, New Delhi : Willey Eastern.

Mathur, V.S., (1983) Value Based Education, *Journal of Indian Education*, 8(5), 31-34.

Mitra, S.K., (1981), Education for National Integration, *University News*, 19(20), 65-66. Moral Science Series Vol. I-VIII, Madras : Macmilan 1974. Neoline, Sister and Martis, D.G. Wonderful life, Series, Part I-X, New Delhi, Neeta Prakashan 1983.

Oad, L.K., (1980-81), Impact of Indian Thought in Developing a Value-pattern in Education, *Journal of Indian Education*, 6(5), 8-12.

Pant, K.C., (1985), Education in Human Values, its Relevance and Strategy, *University News*, 23(31), 2-4.

Paintal, A.S., (1997), Towards Value Education-convocation Address, *University News*, 35(6), 16-19.

Pillai, K.K., (1986), Value-oriented Education, *Journal of Educational Research and Extension*, 22(4).

Piaget, J.M., (1932), *The Moral Judgment of the Child, Pereira*, J.D. Practical Moral Science, Grades I-X, New Delhi: Neeta Prakashan 1982.

Pia Nazareth RJM and Waples Maria, E. Neighbourly Values; Personal Values; Community Values; Values Through Communication–Evaluation Techniques; To

Live or not to Live with Values; (All the five titles were published by the All India Association of Catholic Schools, New Delhi, 1979).

Rajput, J.S., (March 1993), Value Inculcation Through Teacher Training, *University News.*

Rao, K.S., (1995), Value-crisis and the need for value based education, *Journal of Educational Research and Extension*, 32 (1), 41-50.

Ruhela, S.P., (1986), *Human Values and Education*, New Delhi : Sterling, xvi.

Ruhela, S.P., (2000), *Indian Society and Education in 2010*, Delhi : Indian Publishers Distributors.

Saraf, S., (1995), *Education in Human Values, Programme Implementation*, New Delhi : Apeejay Education Foundation, p. 158.

Rama Rao, K., Moral Education : A Practical Approach, Ramakrishna Institute of Moral and Spiritual Education, Mysore 1986. Rohidekar, S.R. *et al.* (Ed.) Education in Human Values : Handbook, for Teachers, Part II, Sri Sathya Sai Bal Vikas Education Trust, Prashanti Nilaya, 1982.

Srinivasa Char, S., (1980), You asked us Ramakrishna Institute of Moral and Spiritual Education, Mysore.

Srivastava, P.R., (1978), Graded Moral Science, Rameshwar Das Gupta Dharmarth Trust, New Delhi.

Sharma, J.N. & Bhatt, P.C., (1992), *Value Education in Our Schools*, New Delhi.

Sarkar, Amit, (1985), *Secularism and Constitution*, New Delhi, p. 79.

Sharma, G.S., (ed.), (1985), *Secularism-Its Implications for Law and Life in India*, ILI, New Delhi.

Sarangi, R., (1994), *Moral Educations in Schools : Bases and Implications*, New Delhi : Deep and Deep.

Sharma, S., (1986), National Integration : Challenge for Teachers, *Bhartiya Adhunik Shiksha* 3(4).

Singh, R., (1987), National Integration and Education, *Bhartiya Adhunik Shiksha* 4(3), 5-8.

Sharma, A.P., (1990), Values Education : A philosophical Perspective, *Journal of Indian Educational* 6(3), 7-10.

Sneh, N.R., (1992), Values in Search of Education, *Journal of Education and Social in Change*, 6 (1), 1-17.

Sharma, R.K., (1996), Development of Moral Education through Social Science Subjects, *Bhartiya Adhunik Shiksha*, 13 (4), 36-37.

Sharma, J.N., (1992), Citizenship Development with Special Emphasis on Value Education, *University News*, 30(24), 8.

Srivastava, P.K., (1969), Age Change in Valuation of Equality, Liberty and Modernity, *Indian Journal of Gerontology*, 1(4), 115-117.

Singh, Gurmukh Nihar, (1985), The Changing Concept of Citizenship, Orient Longmans.

Sharma, A.P., (1990), Values Education: A Philosophical Perspective, *Journal of Indian Educational* 6(3), 7-10.

Sundaran, S., (1990), Need for Moral Education, *Journal of Indian Education*, 15 (5), 1-5.

Tripathy, V.R., (1988). *Human Values through Education. Gujarat Vidyapith* : T.K.N. Unnitham. Textbook on Moral Education for Higher School Classes, Karnataka : Directorate of Textbooks, Banglore, 1973.

Venkataiah, N., (ed.), (1998), *Value Education*, New Delhi: APH Publishing Corporation.

Venkataiah, N., (1993), *Curriculum Innovation for 2000 AD*, New Delhi : Ashish Publishing House.

Verma, Meera, (1988), Psycho Studies (1975), "Moral Development and Intelligence", Venkataramiah, E.S., Citizenship – Rights and Duties, Banglore, p. 32.

## CDS PUBLICATIONS

### IN ENGLISH

1. Good Citizenship–Rights, Duties and Responsibilities.
2. Aging in India–Problems and Potentialities.
3. Citizenship Development and Fundamental Duties : Contains Chapters contributed by eminent persons like Dr. L.M. Singhvi, Shri Ram Krishna Hegde, Justice E.S. Venkataramiah, Former Chief Justice of India and others.
4. Citizenship Development–Western More, Eastern Values, Monograph contains edited versions of the address by Fritiz Bolkestein and Dr. L.M. Singhvi.
5. Citizenship Values in India–Individual and Society, contains contributions from Tata Baig, K.D. Gangrade, Dr. K.B. Lall and others.
6. Teacher's Guide on Value Education.
7. Value Education in our Schools with special reference to strategies for New Education Policy.
8. Democracy and Citizenship–A Treatise to provide background knowledge on Citizenship Development edited by Dr. Atma Ram and Shri J.N. Sharma.
9. Citizens and the Constitution : Dr. Subhash C. Kashyap.
10. Value Education : Shri J.N. Sharma and Dr. K.M. Gupta.
11. Guide for Nursery Teachers by Smt. Kamala Kapur.
12. Rights of Consumer as citizen.
13. Environmental Education.
14. Values Based Customer's Service.
15. Economic Upliftment of Rural Women.
16. Building up Good Citizens.
17. Resource Material on Value Education, Program in School, Mrs. Nirmala Kapur, Joint Director, CRTC.

18. Report on Regional Seminar-Cum-Workshop held at Madras, Guwahati and Goa.
19. Report on Seminar on Gandhian Concept of Human Values, New Delhi.
20. Report on the Seminar-Cum-Workshop on Value Based Customer Service under Bankers Education Programme for officers of the Punjab National Bank.
21. Value Education at Primary School Level–role of DIETs, – Mr. J.N. Sharma, Mr. S.P. Dutta, Prof. B.R. Goyal and Dr. K.M. Gupta.
22. A Handbook for Operationalization of Citizenship Values under the Constitution.

**IN HINDI**

1. Book on New Education Policy (Nai Shiksha Niti Ka Nirman Paddhatiyon Ke Vishesh Sandharbh Main, Hamare School Main Mulyaparak Shiksha).
2. Achhi Nagrikta Ki Sankalpana.
3. Nagrikon Ke Adhikar tatha Kartavya.
4. Hamare Gaon Ka Badalta Swaroop.
5. Report of the Convention of Sarpanches in Panchayati Raj System.
6. Samvindhan aur Aam Admi, Dr. Subhash C. Kashyap.

# Index

C